Twayne's United States Authors Series

Sylvia E. Bowman, *Editor*

INDIANA UNIVERSITY

Katherine Anne Porter

TUSAS 90

KATHERINE ANNE PORTER

by **GEORGE HENDRICK**
University of Illinois, Chicago

TWAYNE PUBLISHERS
A DIVISION OF G. K. HALL & CO., BOSTON

For
Willene

Contents

Preface

KATHERINE ANNE PORTER has had a special place in American literature for over forty years. First hailed for the short stories which were collected in *Flowering Judas*, she added to her reputation with the publication of *Pale Horse, Pale Rider*, which contained three short novels, and *The Leaning Tower*. After decades of work, she finally completed *Ship of Fools*, her first long novel, a best seller in 1962. The actual volume of the artistic work which she has chosen to publish has been relatively small but of extremely high quality.

Miss Porter is a highly personal writer, and this study begins with a brief biographical essay. Miss Porter's life is of great interest to anyone studying her art, but the facts about her are scanty. I have brought together the scattered and often contradictory evidence, but I am fully aware of the incompleteness of this chapter.

In the chapters containing individual discussions of Miss Porter's stories, I pay special attention to the settings, themes, and literary indebtednesses. I have grouped these stories, somewhat arbitrarily, under three headings. In the chapter, "My Familiar Country," I indicate that Miss Porter's artistic use of the Mexican scene changed over the decades, from seeing Mexican culture from the inside in "María Concepción" to the later stories of alienation. The next stories are grouped under the title "The Native Land of My Heart" and are fictionalized autobiography, with the grandmother and Miranda as central characters. I have reordered the stories in order to emphasize the influence of the grandmother and Southern society upon Miranda, who enters the brave new world. In "To Tell a Straight Story," the last of these chapters on the short fiction, I have discussed the stories with Southwestern, universalized, Irish, and German settings, attempting at all times to show Miss Porter's mastery of the short story form.

Because of the mixed critical notices of *Ship of Fools*, I have included a long section of criticism, from America, England, and Germany. When Miss Porter publishes more of her journals, we will understand the characters and political events of this novel much better. I have, however, ventured some speculations on Miss Porter's artistic use of the Mexican dissipations and the death of Hart Crane, but I am confident that, with more information on this period in Miss Porter's life, the Crane episode will undoubtedly appear less startling and will shrink into a more proper perspective. I have attempted to show that this vast and subtle novel, much influenced by Brant, Joyce, and James, is one of the major achievements of our time.

In the chapter on the essays, I pay particular attention to Miss Porter's collected writings in *The Days Before* and to the few published sections of the still uncompleted study of Cotton Mather, which promises to be of major importance.

Miss Porter is a conscious literary artist in the tradition of James and Joyce. Her stories show a mastery of technique, honesty, and an exploration of the human personality and society itself. She has reordered, through art, the disorder of life. She is correct in her self-estimation: she is an artist.

To reduce the number of footnotes, I have appended in the notes at the beginning of each story a list of the criticism I have found most pertinent. I have not given page numbers to quotations from Miss Porter's writings, except for *Ship of Fools,* or to quotations from the criticism, for the stories and the criticism are short and the quotations are easily found.

I am deeply indebted to staff members of the British Museum, the Brownwood, Texas, Public Library, the Fort Worth, Texas, Public Library, the Frankfurt University Library, the University of Texas Library, and the Rowalt Verlag for their help. I was also aided by Betty Dodd, Donna Gerstenberger, Sarah Youngblood, Marc Ratner, Charles Larson, W. C. Pool, M. O. Triesch, James Brannock, and Armin Frank.

I am also indebted to those who have previously written on Miss Porter, for they have consistently written knowledgeable essays on Miss Porter and her art, to my students in Frankfurt who studied Miss Porter's writings with me, and to my wife.

GEORGE HENDRICK

Frankfurt/Main, West Germany
October, 1963
Chicago, Illinois
November, 1964

Chronology

1890 ? Katherine Anne Porter born May 15 in Indian Creek, Texas, daughter of Harrison and Mary Alice Jones Porter.

1892 Death of mother. Family then moved to Kyle, Texas, to be cared for by Harrison Porter's mother, Catherine Anne Porter.

1901 Death of Catherine Anne Porter.

1901- Family farm sold after death of grandmother. Porters
1917 moved to San Antonio in 1903 or 1904. Attended Southern convent schools (?). Ran away from school at sixteen and married; divorced at nineteen. Went to Chicago in 1911 (?) where she "got a newspaper job, and went into the movies." Returned to Texas in 1914 and entertained, singing Scottish ballads in self-made costume. Suspected of having tuberculosis.

1917 Employed on *The Critic*, a weekly newspaper published in Fort Worth.

1918- Reporter on *Rocky Mountain News* in Denver; danger-
1919 ously ill with influenza.

1919 Moved to New York and did hack and ghost writing.

1920 Studied art in Mexico.

1921- Returned to Fort Worth and wrote articles about her
1922 Mexican experiences, supporting herself by writing for a trade magazine. Acted in the Fort Worth Little Theatre. Wrote "María Concepción."

1922- Traveled in Mexico; prepared an exhibit of folk art;
1929 lived in New York and worked on a biography of Cotton Mather; did book reviewing for New York publications.

1930 Published *Flowering Judas*.

1931 Awarded Guggenheim Fellowship and lived in Mexico; Hart Crane her house guest for a short time.

1932 Traveled in Europe after leaving Mexico in 1931. Trip to Germany provided background for *Ship of Fools*.

1933 Married (later divorced) Eugene Pressly, member of the American Foreign Service.

1935 Published enlarged volume of *Flowering Judas*.

1937 Book-of-the-Month Club Award of $2500.

1938 Married Albert Erskine, Jr., of the Louisiana State University faculty; divorced, 1942.

1939 Published *Pale Horse, Pale Rider*.

1942 Translated and wrote introduction to José Joaquín Fernández de Lizárdi's *The Itching Parrot*.

1943 Elected member of National Institute of Arts and Letters.

1944 Published *The Leaning Tower and Other Stories*.

1949- Guest lecturer at Stanford University, University of
1962   Chicago, University of Michigan, University of Liège, University of Virginia, Washington and Lee University, and many other colleges and universities.

1952 Published *The Days Before*.

1962 Published *Ship of Fools*, an immediate best seller. Now lives in Washington, D.C.

Katherine Anne Porter

CHAPTER 1

The Fiery Furnace and After

K ATHERINE ANNE PORTER often speaks of the relationship between her past and her art; typical of these statements is one made at La Salle College in 1961 when she said, "My safety ground as a writer is based on what I saw or heard or experienced, a reality which I never get mixed up with fiction, only elaborate on."[1] In her journal for 1936 she wrote that the "exercise of memory" is "the chief occupation of my mind, and all my experience seems to be simply memory, with continuity, marginal notes, constant revision and comparison of one thing with another. Now and again thousands of memories converge, harmonize, arrange themselves around a central idea in a coherent form, and I write a story."[2]

Obviously, then, Miss Porter's biography is of value to anyone interested in her art, but she has been extremely reticent in revealing biographical information, especially about her early years. Even the date of her birth is something of a mystery; for years she listed 1894, but recently she has been giving 1890. She has said rather vaguely that she attended small Southern convent schools, but we do not know which ones or for how long. Even her childhood religion is in doubt—her fictional family in the Miranda stories is Catholic, and her biographical sketches speak of her education in Catholic schools—but Texans who knew her as a child insist that the Porters were Methodists. Ray B. West, in early studies of Miss Porter and in his recent pamphlet *Katherine Anne Porter*, accepted the fictional Catholicism as fact and interpreted many of her stories in terms of the moral values of Catholicism; this interpretation was not challenged until recently, when Miss Porter asked Professor West to enter a correction about her religion in the University of Minnesota pamphlet. Just when Miss Porter was converted is not now known; one of my informants thinks it was after her bout with influenza in Denver in 1918. Many years of her life, especially those before 1930, are not accounted for at all in the biographical sketches she provided for *Who's Who in America, Twentieth Century Authors,* and *Current Biography.*

Miss Porter wrote in "Reflections on Willa Cather," that she has little interest in biography after the tenth year, for what is to be is determined by then: "The rest is merely confirmation, extension, development. Childhood is the fiery furnace in which we are melted down to essentials and that essential shaped for good." Until the Porter family papers, if they exist, and Miss Porter's own manuscripts and papers become available, it is not possible to study in detail this formative period of her life. But from scattered biographical statements, the pioneering master's thesis of Mr. Donald Stalling,[3] who interviewed elderly Texans who had known the Porters, and from my own interviews in 1962, part of this past can be reconstructed.

I *The Family*

Miss Porter's maternal ancestors settled in 1648 in "John Randolph territory of Virginia." She told the *Paris Review,* in an interview published in the Winter-Spring, 1963, issue, that one of her great-great-grandfathers was Jonathan Boone, Daniel's brother. In early accounts, Miss Porter spoke of Daniel as the ancestor, but she has recently set the record straight. In the *Paris Review* interview, she implies that the Boone relations were on her mother's side, not her father's, as she presents them in the Miranda stories. Of her father's family, which appears more often in the fiction, she has said that Andrew Porter came to Pennsylvania in 1720, was "one of the circle of Gen. George Washington during the Revolution, a friend of Lafayette," and a founder of the Society of Cincinnati. She ended the genealogy by saying that, though there was a "desire to excel," the family was not ambitious, probably because "We thought we'd *already* arrived!" Her paternal grandparents were Asbury and Catherine Anne Porter. The Porter family moved to Kyle, Texas, after the Civil War; in the fictional account, the grandfather died before that emigration, although the tombstone in Kyle gives his death as 1879. Mrs. Porter struggled in this raw, crude country to maintain the genteel traditions of her youth in Kentucky. The family was land poor and had no prospects of economic inprovement, but the house was "full of books—a roomful called a library, and books lying on every chair and table."[4] Miss Porter explained in "Portrait: Old South" that they "had been a good old family of solid wealth and property" in the South and they "remained that in Texas, even though due to a temporary decline" in fortunes, "appearances were entirely to the contrary."

When Miss Porter's father Harrison (he is called Harry in the Miranda stories) married Mary Alice Jones about 1880, they settled in Indian Creek in Brown County, a section of the state even more primitive than Kyle. Miss Porter was the third of five children, four of whom, according to Stalling, survived. During her childhood, she was called "Callie," and old-time residents in Indian Creek and Kyle almost always refer to her by this name. She was a beautiful child, but Miss McAden, an elderly resident in Indian Creek, told Mr. Stalling that "at the age of four she was still a big baby." "I wouldn't say she was spoiled," Miss McAden said, "but when she wanted something, she wouldn't give an inch until she got it. And if she wanted something, she would keep working until she got it."

This intransigence seems to have been inherited from her grandmother. Miss Posey, one of Alice Porter's friends, told Stalling that when flowers, ordered for a social Grandmother Porter was sponsoring in San Marcos, did not arrive, she drove her horses in a gallop to Austin and back to get them. "The two horses dropped dead when she drove up at San Marcos, but she did not show a flicker of regret. She got what she wanted when she wanted it." The story may well be apocryphal, but the grandmother was obviously a woman of great determination. Miss Porter's summary of her own temperament agrees with the memories of the elderly women in Indian Creek: "I was precocious, nervous, rebellious, unteachable, and made life very uncomfortable for myself and I suppose for those around me."[5]

Mary Alice Porter died in 1892—two years before Miss Porter's birth, according to all but the most recent biographical dictionaries—soon after giving birth to her fifth child, and about a year later Harrison Porter moved his children to Kyle to be reared by the grandmother. In Indian Creek then, Miss Posey remembered, "the cattle business was about the only business people knew," but Kyle was much more settled and cultured by this time. Fellow Southerners were well established, and the Porters even had on their property some of their ex-slaves. For the next few years the children were dominated by the willful grandmother who rode horseback until the year she died and who had to be restrained from changing the course of a river which threatened to damage her property.

Mrs. Porter had a farm outside of Kyle, and she seems to have divided her time between her town house in Kyle and the farm. She was a strict disciplinarian, ruling the children with precepts such as "Children should be seen and not heard" and "Handsome is as handsome does."[6]

Miss Porter remembers that, as soon as she learned to form letters, at about the age of three, she began to write. In an interview with Archer Winsten, published in the New York *Post*, May 6, 1937, she said that when she was six, "She wrote, bound and hand-printed what she called 'A Nobbel—The Hermit of Halifax Cave.'" Writing became her "basic and absorbing occupation, the intact line" of her life. Some of her early stories may have been dramatized, for a Kyle resident told Stalling about walking by grandmother Porter's house and seeing "the yard . . . full of children watching or participating in a drama directed by the granddaughter Callie."

After the grandmother died in 1901, the family broke up, and a family acquaintance told Mr. Stalling that Harrison Porter and the children lived a gypsy life, moving about from place to place without a home. After the farm and town house in Kyle were sold, Miss Porter remembers, the family moved late in 1903 or early in 1904 to San Antonio. Miss Posey told Stalling that in 1906 Miss Porter had a great desire to go on the stage and "was studying dramatics in some school there in San Antonio." Was this perhaps one of the convent schools she attended? One friend of Miss Porter has suggested she was enrolled in Catholic schools because they were cheaper than the Protestant boarding schools. At any rate, she was an indifferent student, Glenway Wescott reported in *Images of Truth;* she made excellent marks in history, literature, and composition, but "D" in everything else except deportment, which was often lower.

In the *Paris Review* interview, Miss Porter commented on her reading at this time: "That was the turning point of my life, when I read the Shakespeare sonnets, and then, all at one blow, all of Dante—in that great big book illustrated by Gustave Doré." In addition, she read Homer, Ronsard, "all the old French poets in translation," Montaigne, Voltaire's "philosophical dictionary with notes by Smollett," the eighteenth-century novelists, Dickens, and Thackeray. Her grandmother did not approve of the modern writers: "she thought Dickens might do, but she was a little against Mr. Thackeray; she thought he was too trivial. So that was as far as I got into the modern world until I left home!"

When she was sixteen, Miss Porter ran away from the convent school and married; three years later she was divorced. The next year she left Texas, because "I didn't want to be regarded as a freak. That was how they regarded a woman who tried to write. I had to make a revolt, a rebellion. . . . When I left they were all certain I was going to live an immoral life. It was a confining society in those days." She told Archer Winsten that she had written of that society in "Legend and Memory," the first part of a novel which was to be called "Many Redeemers"; but this fiction has not been published, at least not under these titles.

II *Early Career*

In Chicago she found a job on a newspaper and worked as an extra in a film studio, but she refused to go with the company to Hollywood, for she knew what luxury would do for her, knew that she was corruptible. Desperately poor, intent on making her own way, Miss Porter said in 1937 that she often went without food, developed tuberculosis (according to some recollections in Indian Creek, Mrs. Harrison Porter was tubercular), and returned to Texas.[7]

In the interview from the *Paris Review,* Miss Porter told a slightly different story:

> The newspaper sent me over to the old S. and A. movie studio to do a story. But I got into the wrong line, and then was too timid to get out. "Right over this way, Little Boy Blue," the man said, and I found myself in a courtroom scene with Francis X. Bushman. I was horrified by what had happened to me, but they paid me $5 for that first day's work, so I stayed on. It was about a week before I remembered what I had been

sent to do, and when I went back to the newspaper they gave me $18 for my week's non-work and fired me!

I stayed on for six months—I finally got to nearly $10 a day—until one day they came in and said, "We're moving to the coast." "Well I'm not," I said. "Don't you want to be a movie actress?" "Oh no!" I said. "Well, be a fool!" he said, and left. That was 1914 and World War had broken out, so in September I went home.

Interviewer: "And then?"

"Oh, I sang old Scottish ballads in costume—I made it myself—all around Texas and Louisiana. And then I was supposed to have TB, and spent about six weeks in a sanitarium. It was just bronchitis, but I was in Denver, so I got a newspaper job. . . ."

The difficulty of treating this—in fact, virtually every—period of Miss Porter's life is admirably stated by Glenway Wescott, who observed in *Images of Truth* that Miss Porter tends to "simplify" for those who ask questions about her life: "And therefore I (and other friends)," he remarks, "instead of concentrating on ascertaining all the realities, the dates and the names and the locations and so on, have always interested ourselves in what might be called story-material about her, somehow more characteristic than her mere biography."

Mr. Wescott then gives an example of this "story material," an incident which seemingly follows her stay in Chicago: While she was a girl "somewhere in the South" she spent months in a sanitarium with one of the "uncommon forms of tuberculosis." Books, letters, and visitors were forbidden because they excited her; finally the doctor ordered that her eyes be covered with a green cloth several hours a day, for her restless eyes gave her a temperature. The incident, Mr. Wescott suggests, was "the beginning of a lifetime of delicate health and indomitable strength."[8] The tone of the anecdote has all of the elements of mystery and shadow which Miss Porter uses to surround her nonfictional presentation of her past.

III *The Preparation of a Writer*

Miss Porter's movements during the next ten years are almost completely unknown. Although she planned to be a writer, she exiled herself from literary centers, prolonging her apprenticeship as an artist but saving herself from discipleship. These were apparently years of great intellectual ferment. She told Margaret Marshall that Shakespeare's sonnets were for her a "reality" at fourteen and at fifteen she read the great Russian novelists; at the same time, she was "imitating" Laurence Sterne. She reported in *Twentieth Century Authors* that, until she was twenty-five, she concentrated on English and Continental classics and then began on the newcomers. She discovered Willa Cather's *O Pioneers!* (1913) soon after it appeared and continued to read Miss Cather's novels as they were published. Along with *O Pioneers!* she was also reading Henry James, W. B. Yeats, and Joseph Conrad. Gertrude Stein's *Tender Buttons* brought on the beginning of her quarrel with what Miss Porter calls the school of modern writing "in which poverty of feeling and idea were disguised, but not well enough, in tricky techniques and disordered syntax." A year or so later she discovered by accident, in a small Texas town, Joyce's *Dubliners*, which came to her not as a shock but as a revelation, a "further unfolding of the deep world of the imagination."

In "It Is Hard to Stand in the Middle" Miss Porter expanded the list of contemporary writers who had influenced her to include T. S. Eliot and Ezra Pound, and she added that the beginning writer is educated by the artist who shows him how "to work his own vein, who helps him to fix his standards, and who gives him courage." Katherine Mansfield, Thomas Hardy, E. M. Forster, and Virginia Woolf were also important writers for Miss Porter, as the essays in *The Days Before* clearly show.[9]

Friends who knew her just before World War I described her to Paul Crume: "a pretty girl . . . with a round face and violet eyes and curly dark hair, hard and slim of body from much dancing and swimming, impulsively generous, friendly."[10] Sometime in 1917 she arrived in Fort Worth, Texas, where she worked as a reporter on *The Critic*, a weekly tabloid devoted to politics, drama, business, and local events. She wrote drama criticism and society gossip. She was, undoubtedly from necessity, following the advice which Miranda ignored in "Pale Horse, Pale Rider"; "All you have to do is play up the headliners, and you needn't even mention the also-rans. Try to keep in mind that Rypinsky has got show business cornered in this town;

please Rypinsky and you'll please the advertising department, please them and you'll get a raise. Hand-in-glove, my poor dumb child, will you never learn?" She wrote in *The Critic* of the local vaudeville house: "We can't have too much good vaudeville for the soldier boys, and the Byyers management is giving us the best—clean, original, with plenty of comedy. A commendable evenness of quality is maintained from week to week, and the bills are well balanced." Her first gossip column was appropriately addle-headed, filled with news of war work, the local music club which was organizing "Sing Songs where the boys may harmonize together quite chummily," and fashion notes. (In the *Paris Review* interview she indicated that it was better for a writer to work as waitress than as newspaperwoman; it was better to take dull jobs that would not take all her mind or time.)

Although *The Critic* caption under Miss Porter's picture announcing her joining the staff declared that she planned to devote her life to the newspaper,[11] she stayed only a short time; and in 1918 she became a reporter on the *Rocky Mountain News* in Denver, Colorado. Some stories indicate that Miss Porter feared her lungs were still weak and therefore sought the mountain climate. Whatever the reasons for her flight to the West, she was there for only a few months, for she was a victim of the influenza epidemic of 1918 and almost died.

Kathryn Sexton, preparing a master's thesis on Miss Porter, interviewed Denverites who had known Miss Porter and found one co-worker on the *Rocky Mountain News* who remembered her as "glamorous and intriguing," a slim young woman who habitually wore gray clothes and a gray hood pulled up over her head—for her hair had come out during her illness. Just when Miss Porter began work on the *News* is not known, but between February 18 and August 17, 1919, she contributed eighty-one signed articles, including movie, drama, and vaudeville reviews; musical criticism; and interviews. Characteristically, she found that most of the drama of the time was "mostly a libel on life, on art, on . . . morals."

Much of this journalistic writing is of little literary interest, but one does find at times such ironic, satiric statements as, "A play once ran forty-seven—or seventy-four weeks in New York. It was an unusually awful play, and therefore was unusually popular. Backed by these weeks—47 or 74—it started a career of crime across the country and finally arrived in the West. Here in a certain city in the foothills it struck a snag in the form of a lowly critic who hadn't noticed, or didn't care, if the play ran all those months in New York. . . . she up and said this play was inadequate"; and, as a result, the actors, actors' friends, and her own friends acted as if all the hyenas of the Rockies had broken loose.

She also acted in little theater groups, playing the swallow in Oscar Wilde's *The Happy Prince,* and a pot in an Omar Khayyam pageant.[12]

Those whom Mrs. Sexton interviewed felt that "Pale Horse, Pale Rider" was autobiographic, and they could recognize certain scenes, incidents, and characters; but they could not illuminate the personality of Miss Porter: she was too isolated, too withdrawn from them. Everything they reported about Miss Porter, about Denver during the last months of the war, and about the *Rocky Mountain News* staff seems stale in comparison with Miss Porter's distillation in "Pale Horse, Pale Rider" of her own personality, the time, and the place. One friend who knew her just before and after World War I told Paul Crume, "She doesn't wait for death to effect transmigration. Every now and then she stops being what she is and becomes something else. In some secluded corner of the world, she spins a cocoon, and presently comes out more brilliantly colored, with longer, swifter wings. She leaves her old life there in a tree, dry and forgotten and dead, something she has put forever behind her."[13]

After recovering from influenza, Miss Porter went to New York and took on another life. She lived in the Village and supported herself by doing ghost writing, work which frightened her, she told Van Gelder; for it seemed unbelievable that anyone would want to sign a book he had not written. Her best-known ghosted work is *My Chinese Marriage* by M. T. F. (1921). Miss Porter wrote Edward Schwartz when he was compiling "A Critical Bibliography" of her works that the ghosted books "should have no place in the list of my works."[14]

She stayed only a short time in New York before going to Mexico where she apparently planned to work with those organizing the new labor government. In the *Paris Review* interview, she says that Mexican artists in New York kept talking about the renaissance in Mexico and told her to go there instead of Europe because, they said, "that's where the exciting things are going to happen." She did go, just in time to witness the Obregón Revolution; and she had "the most marvelous, natural, spontaneous experience of my life. . . . It was alive, but death was in it. But nobody seemed to think of that: life was in it, too."

Again she remained only briefly, returning to Forth Worth, where she began writing her impressions of Mexico, including "María Concepción," which she says she rewrote fifteen or sixteen times. She supported herself by writing for a trade paper owned by the publisher of *The Critic* and also found time to act with local drama groups. She sold "María Concepción" and non-fiction works on Mexico to *Century Magazine* and returned to Mexico, this time interested in folk art; she arranged an American exhibit of Mexican art and later wrote *Outline of Mexican Popular Arts and Crafts*. During the middle 1920's she also did extensive book reviewing for the New York *Herald Tribune, The New Republic,* and *The Nation.* These were years of constant travel; but, until her notebooks and correspondence are published, the exact itinerary and dates cannot be known.

Her short stories appeared infrequently, but by 1930 she had chosen for publication—after throwing away trunkfuls of her stories, she has said—enough stories to form the slim volume *Flowering Judas,* which established her critical reputation. The next year she received a Guggenheim award and spent the year in Mexico. During this time she had a traumatic experience with Hart Crane, who did not, as most of her friends have done, protect her private life. Crane, also awarded a Guggenheim that year, went to Mexico and was invited to stop with Miss Porter; but, according to Philip Horton, Crane's first biographer, she soon regretted the invitation because of the excesses in his personal life. Finally forced to move, he rented the house next door. Invited to a dinner party at his house which she did not attend, Miss Porter was later that night cursed by the drunken Crane, a scene she describes in a detailed letter quoted by Horton.[15]

Crane himself wrote of the incident in a letter, saying she did not reply to his apology and adding as a last note: "It's all very sad and disagreeable. But one imputation I won't stand for. That is the obvious and usual one: that my presence in the neighborhood was responsible for a break or discontinuance of Katherine Anne's creative work. . . . I'm tired of being made into a bogey or ogre rampant in Mexico and tearing the flesh of delicate ladies. I'm also tired of a certain rather southern type of female vanity. And that's about all I ever want to say about Katherine Anne again personally."[16] Crane's behavior was undoubtedly outrageous and disgusting, but he does—in his anger and in his madness—strip away some of the secrecy around Miss Porter's life and reveal her as her grandmother's child, with a fixed moral code and definite ideas on right and wrong sexual and moral behavior.

Almost all critical articles on her works base their biographical information on facts which Miss Porter has given either in interviews or in autobiographical sketches. She has, as Whitman did, attempted to control her own public image. Her abilities as a myth-maker are formidable. In 1940 when "Promised Land" (as *Ship of Fools* was then known) was supposedly nearing completion, she told Robert Van Gelder that formerly she traveled with a suitcase for her personal effects and a steamer trunk for her manuscripts, and that she had burned four novels and many short stories, keeping enough work to occupy her for years: "There are notes for novels, for a biography of Cotton Mather, and for some forty short stories." But in the two decades following this interview, Miss Porter has published only a few of the stories, postponing the Cotton Mather study ("this is more or less like my knitting, to mull over when I get to be eighty," she said in another interview in 1940)[17] year by year, just as she postponed *Ship of Fools* until 1962.

Miss Porter was again announcing her novel in interviews published in *Newsweek* and *Time* in July of 1961, referring to it as "the end of a very prolonged pregnancy," and blaming publishers for all the publicity: "I was nagged and nagged and nagged to finish it. All this pressure to complete a novel—I think it's foolish. You write as much as you can, and you finish as soon as you can, as circumstances permit." This half-defiant—yet fully warranted, in terms of her artistic achievement—justification of her slim literary production has been standard in her interviews for more than twenty years. In 1961 she was still referring to her forty unfinished short stories.[18] Curiously enough, she said in the *Newsweek* interview that she did not begin serious work on the novel until 1941—a year after she told Van Gelder it would be completed. Even the last three decades provide little concrete information about her; she left Mexico for Europe. She had been somewhat disillusioned and distressed during her years in Mexico, for she said in an interview published in the February, 1963, *College English* that she had seen "clowns like Hitler" there (and later in Europe) and, "I was struck by an idea: What if people like this could take over the world! Of course there were all the good worthy people who didn't believe in the clowns, but these good worthy people still let the clowns commit all the crimes good worthy people would commit if only they had the nerve." In Mexico, however, "there was always some *chance* of salvation."

Her voyage to Europe provides the background for *Ship of Fools*. In Berlin she met Goebbels, Goering, and Hitler, all of whom she thought "detestable and dangerous."[19] She married Eugene Pressly, a member of the American Foreign Service, lived in Paris for several years, and published a French song book. During the 1930's, she was attracted to Marxism, she told Archer Winsten in 1937; but she was "afraid for her mental freedom: 'Why should I have rebelled against my early training in Jesuit Catholicism only to take another yoke now?'" Divorced, she married Albert Erskine, Jr., of the Louisiana State University staff and lived in Baton Rouge for several years. Now divorced again, she has spent the last years lecturing, writing movie scripts in Hollywood, serving as artist-in-residence at numerous American colleges and universities, and completing *Ship of Fools*.

Her three volumes of collected stories, one novel, and one volume of collected essays have earned her the highest critical adulation. Robert Penn Warren considers many of her stories "unsurpassed in modern fiction," and he places her in the company of Joyce, Hemingway, Katherine Mansfield, and Sherwood Anderson.[20]

Her creative work is more interesting than the mysteries which surround her, although not, one hastily adds, than her actual life. Glenway Wescott writes rather obliquely of her "vicissitudes" and "personal weaknesses," but Miss Porter's life, for all of its fascination, is reflected in her work. To know her work is to know at least a part of her life and a great deal of her times. As she wrote in the Introduction to *Flowering Judas:* her stories are mere fragments of a much larger plan she is still working on, and they should stand as what she was "able to achieve in the way of order and form and statement in a period of grotesque dislocations in a whole society when the world was heaving in the sickness of a millennial change."

CHAPTER *2*

My Familiar Country

I WRITE ABOUT MEXICO because that is my familiar country," Miss Porter began in "Why I Write about Mexico," a letter to *The Century* in 1923. As a child, she had heard stories about that country from her father (in "Old Mortality" a shooting incident caused Miranda's father to flee to Mexico); she had lived near San Antonio, a Spanish-American center; and Mexico had never seemed strange to her. During the Madero revolution, she viewed the battle in Mexico City and later saw the dead piled in the public square. An old Indian woman who stood watching with her remarked that the revolution was worth all the trouble because of future happiness—and happiness of men, not angels.

After this conversation, the political events which followed— the counterrevolution of Huerta and the assassination of Madero; Carranza's revolutionary movement which resulted in a new constitution providing for badly needed labor, religious, and land reforms; Carranza's assassination in 1920; the coming to power of Obregón's government which began to institute the reforms of the constitution—did not seem false, aimless, or alien.

According to her interview with Archer Winsten in 1937, Miss Porter went to Mexico in 1920 to study art; but, as Winsten paraphrased her remarks, she "found herself instead in the center of the Revolution. Being something of a rebel in her own quiet way, it was easy to plunge in on the side of Liberty, Equality and Fraternity. She taught dancing and physical culture in four of the new schools." In the *Paris Review* interview, Miss Porter spoke of "that wild escapade to Mexico, where I attended, you might say, and assisted at, in my own modest way, a revolution."

Her stories about Mexico, she said in the letter to *The*

Century, were "fragments, each one touching some phase of a versatile national temperament, which is a complication of simplicities: but I like best the quality of aesthetic magnificences, and, above all, the passion for individual expression without hypocrisy, which is the true genius of the race." Her view of art was a natural outgrowth of this belief, for she saw that the renaissance of Mexican art was natural instead of artificial, that it was "unfolding in a revolution which returned to find its freedoms in profound and honorable sources."

Her passionate concern for the Mexican revolution was demonstrated in a series of essays which ran counter to the usual cliché-filled, propagandistic attacks in the popular American press. In "The Mexican Trinity" (1921) she was explicit in her analysis of the foreign and native enemies of the revolution: the Mexican and American capitalists, the landowners, and the Church—all were subjugating the Indian; the country was in the grip of "Oil, Land, and the Church." The most extreme radical group, with its many idealists, was tragic because its cause was hopeless; some groups wanted to begin by correcting the most horrible excesses of the old system, but many of the revolutionists merely followed a leader who was not intent upon reforms but upon establishing himself in power. She was acutely aware that the revolution had yet to enter "the souls of the Mexican people," largely because the intellectuals were still writing romances; even if the intellectuals had cried out against abuses, the Indians could not read. She continued this analysis in "Where Presidents Have No Friends" (1922) with an account of Obregón's attempt to break up the ruling Oil-Church-Land clique and free fifteen. million Mexicans from "poverty, illiteracy, a most complete spiritual and mental darkness...."

From these essays, one would imagine that Miss Porter might have turned to propagandistic fiction, but such was not the case. Mexico was the background for her earliest stories, but she did not attempt, through fiction, to offer solutions to the economic and social problems of that country. The very basis of her art was quite different, as she explained in "No Plot, My Dear, No Story": "have faith in your theme; then get so well acquainted with your characters that they live and grow in your imagination exactly as if you saw them in the flesh; and finally, tell their story with all the truth and tenderness and severity you are capable of; and if you have any character of your own, you will have a style of your own; it grows, as your ideas grow, and as your knowledge of your craft increases."

I *Inside the Mexican Culture*

"María Concepción"

The first fragment of national life which Miss Porter chose to write about was that of the still-primitive Indian. The central theme of "María Concepción"[1] (1922) is the strength of life over defeated death, illustrated in María Concepción's treatment of the chickens, in the Indians' unconcern for their buried past, in María Concepción's reasons for murdering María Rosa, and in the protection she is then given by her husband and by the Indian women.

The opening scene is a brilliant and characteristic performance by Miss Porter; her first published story, it demonstrates a complete grasp of technique. María Concepción, wife of Juan the head digger at the excavations at the buried city, was hurrying down a path which ran through magueys and cactus with their painful thorns and spines, to take noonday food to her young husband and his employer. The heat, the dust, the lonely, forbidding landscape, are superbly drawn, as is María Concepción, pregnant, walking carefully to keep from stepping on thorns. A proud descendant of the race only partially integrated into Mexican life, she was carrying a dozen live chickens over her shoulder, chickens on the way to market and to death. They peered at her inquiringly, but she gave no thought to them or to their fate.

From the first scene, Miss Porter introduces the reader to the ironic distance between things as they are and as they should be, between truth and fiction, between expectation and fulfillment, between art and life. She lays bare the ambiguities of life; and, as Robert Penn Warren has aptly remarked, it is irony with a center. María Concepción, hearing and smelling the bees kept by fifteen-year-old María Rosa, felt that if she did not have a crust of honey, the baby would be marked; and what she saw, as she looked through the cactus, marked her baby and María Rosa for death.

Peering through the cactus hedge, she could see the golden shimmer of the bees, could hear María Rosa's laughter. She smiled to think of María Rosa's having a man; but, when the man appeared, it was her man—a game-cock of a man, flourishing his hat as he went through the ritual of seduction. She did not interfere; but, driven by duty, she went on to the buried city, her ears strumming, as if the bees were in her head, her body burning as if cactus spines were under her skin. The bees and the spines, natural, familiar objects, had instantaneously become sinister, taking on their most painful characteristics.

At first she wanted to die, but not until she had cut the throats of the lovers kissing and laughing under the cornstalks. María Rosa, she thought, was her enemy—a whore with no right to live; and the mere fact that she herself had struggled even less when Juan had first seduced her was meaningless—for they had later been married in the church.

Before she could go on with her bloody thoughts, she saw Givens, no doubt patterned on Miss Porter's friend Niven whose one interest in life was "digging up buried Indian cities all over the country." In "The Charmed Life" Miss Porter says that his monomania made him appealingly unhuman; she accompanied him on expeditions, observing his independent existence: "He ate carelessly at odd hours, fried beans and tortillas from a basket left for him by the wife of his head digger. . . ."[2] Givens was perfectly incomprehensible to the Indians, for he was overjoyed at the pottery fragments, the bits from painted walls, the small clay heads, the human skulls he found in the excavation. The Indians were puzzled by his delight at finding fragments of the past culture, for they could make better pottery for sale to the tourists. Many of them made what money they had by digging in the crevasses which crisscrossed the land like the gashes of a great scalpel.

María Concepción and Givens were completely unable to understand one another; she regarded him condescendingly because he had no woman to cook for him—here we see her concept of what was natural and inevitable in the social order—and he preferred Indians for whom "he could feel a fatherly indulgence for their primitive childish ways." He could understand their past but not their present; they were contemptuous of these artifacts of the past and intent upon life in the present.

For years he had been rescuing Juan from all sorts of escapades and had often warned Juan that María Concepción would discover his infidelities. Givens was blissfully unaware of the tensions within María Concepción as she dressed the chicken he selected, "twisting the head off with the casual firmness she might use with the top of a beet."

Juan did not return to his wife, to the strict young woman who had insisted on a wedding in the church, but fled with María Rosa, for whom work amongst the sweet of the honey was a way of life. They joined the nearest army; obviously, this Don Juan was more concerned with escape than with the aims of his commander or whatever the army was fighting for or against.

María Concepción's child died soon after birth; and, although she spent long hours in church, she was "blind-looking." The butchering knife was almost always in hand. Lupe, the medicine woman and godmother of María Rosa, reported, "She is mere stone." And, when she told María Concepción of praying for her, María Concepción ordered her to pray for those in need: "I will ask God for what I want in this world." Later, however, in avenging herself on María Rosa, she sets herself up as a goddess, decreeing death and taking for her own the newborn baby.

When Juan and María Rosa returned a year later, Juan, dressed in the multi-colored finery taken from dead soldiers, looked and behaved like a cock. Arrested for desertion, he was saved from execution by Givens. María Rosa gave birth to his son, and Juan, confident that he could manage the two women, stood drinks for everyone at the "Death and Resurrection" pulque shop, looked in upon his new son, and later in a drunken stupor attempted to beat María Concepción, to become again the master of his household. She resisted, even struck back; and he fell into a drunken sleep in a corner.

After refusing to be subdued, María Concepción bound the legs of her dumb chickens as if to go to market; but, instead of taking the path, she ran stumblingly through the fields, through the established pattern of Indian agricultural life—her confused psychological state is objectified in her stumbling and running through the plowed and ordered fields. She ran unknowingly until at last she regained possession of herself and knew what she wanted to do. Her new-found knowledge was at first shocking, and she sat in the shade of a thorn-filled bush, giving way "to her long devouring sorrow." She sat, sweat pouring from her, as if all past wounds "were shedding their salt ichor." Reboza drawn over her head which rested on drawn-up knees, she was a figure of sorrow, consumed by anger and grief. The ichor image is particularly significant, because *ichor* is also the ethereal fluid of the gods. When she arose, she no longer ran stumblingly but walked.

It is clear in Miss Porter's story that this seemingly primitive society with its own order, its own morality, its own ethic, was being encroached upon by a harsh Nature, a Western religion, and the more sophisticated society of the outside world. María Concepción could re-establish order in her own world only by breaking outwardly imposed restraints, by becoming a goddess dispensing justice.

The actual murder and the flight of María Concepción are not described; the scene shifts to Juan's being wakened from his drunken stupor by noises he could not comprehend. María Concepción loomed in the doorway, knife in hand, then crawled toward him as she had previously crawled toward a shrine; he was, in fact, a kind of God for her, and she had quickly put away her earlier desire to kill him. Juan at first feared for his own safety; but, when he heard her story, he felt immense pride and a desire to protect her. He went through a carefully reasoned plan of cleansing her and the knife. The scene is played in the dark—María Rosa had been killed about sundown—then in flickering candlelight. The dangers of the night were everywhere, but Juan prepared the poor creature, the madwoman as he called her, for the police. He threatened, in his awakening manly responsibility, to settle accounts with her after she was safe; but she replied, with the charcoal burner casting a yellow glimmer behind the iris of her eyes, that all was settled. Juan knew it was true and wanted to repent not as a man but as a child; he could not understand her or himself, or life itself—life now confused when in former times it had seemed simple.

That night they ate from the same bowl, as they had before his flight, symbolizing their reunion; and, when the police came, Juan began his public defense of his wife. At Lupe's house, where they were taken for the interrogation, the body of María

Rosa lay in an open coffin; she was covered with a rose reboza, but María Concepción could see María Rosa's scarred feet which were similar to the swollen feet of the death-marked chickens María Concepción could not see. She was no longer afraid, no longer angry at the pitiable creature in the coffin: "María Rosa had eaten too much honey and had had too much love. Now she must sit in hell, crying over her sins and her hard death forever and ever."

Old Lupe knew the truth but enjoyed outwitting the police, enjoyed her moment of glory while being questioned, enjoyed describing the evil-sounding footsteps. She was intensely aware of the rôle she played as medicine woman, a sophisticated rôle in a primitive society; the police were aware of the part she was playing, but could do nothing.

María Rosa had been rejected in death, and the Indians embraced life. As María Concepción looked around the circle, the eyes which met hers were filled with reassurance, understanding, and sympathy. Absolved, María Concepción took as her natural right the child which lay at the head of the coffin, new life juxtaposed with almost forgotten death. María Rosa, destined for the grave, was to become a part of their buried past.

Juan was sentenced to life in the dead city. His fate was, in some ways, more tragic than María Concepción's. Even before the murder, when he was being held for desertion, the officer looked at him in his flamboyant costume and saw nothing. As a Don Juan, he was a vacuum; forced into maturity by the murder of his mistress and by the defense of his wife, he still had no strength. Sentenced to dull, senseless labor, from which he saw no escape, he accepted his fate. He did not understand his actions of the day, felt only a "blind hurt like a covered wound." Significantly, he did not ponder his fate, but went to sleep, first symbolically throwing off his vari-colored clothes, the outward sign of his destroyed, unfettered life.

María Concepción's world was now aright. She milked the goat, maternally letting the kid suckle briefly, and fed the baby, a baby she dreamed was hers. Family had won over love; life had won over death.

Miss Porter in the story introduces a series of opposites: the buried life—the present, the light—the dark, Christianity— Paganism, American—Indian, love—duty, walking—stumbling, honey—thorns. Constantly shifting from one opposite to another, from one point of view to another, Miss Porter plunges the reader into the amoral-moral world of the Indian, and by extension plumbs the basis of all human existence. In this, her first story, she sees that order is imposed only through reordering or destroying the order-disorder of others.

"The Martyr"

The two Mexican stories which followed, "The Martyr" (*The Century Magazine*, July, 1923) and "Virgin Violeta" (*The Century Magazine*, December, 1924), are inferior to "María Concepción," and Miss Porter has not included them in her collected stories. In "The Martyr" she portrays ironically an artist who gives himself to self-pity after his model leaves him for another artist. Rubén, the greatest artist of Mexico, completed for a mural, drawing after drawing of his mistress Isabel, before her other lover sold a painting, which was fortunately the right color for a wall, and took her away. Rubén became a martyr to love—could think of nothing, could talk of nothing except the simple-minded girl whose new love would never make her cook and would buy her a pair of red shoes. To ease his pain, he consumed great quantities of food and drink and grew ludicrously fat. A doctor, sent by friends, prescribes, in a wildly comic scene, diet, long walks, exercise, cold baths, as a cure for the wounded heart; but Rubén could only murmur, romantically, that Isabel was his executioner, that he would soon be in his narrow, dark grave.

Deserted by his friends, Rubén finally died of a seizure at "The Little Donkeys" restaurant where he was dining. The friends, who had fled his tiring stories about Isabel, reappeared. The owner of the restaurant confided to the artist Ramón, who would write the biography of Rubén, illustrating it with his own character sketches, that Rubén's last words had been: "Tell them I am a martyr to love. I perish in a cause worthy the sacrifice. I die of a broken heart! Isabelita, my executioner!" Ramón told the proprietor the last words "should be very eloquent," for they would "add splendor to the biography, nay, to the very history of art itself, if they are eloquent." The proprietor, who may or may not have heard the final words he quotes, emphasized that the great artist had been inordinately fond of the tamales served in the restaurant. They were "his final indulgence." The story ends on the same ironic note: " 'That shall be mentioned in its place, never fear, my good friend,' cried Ramón, his voice crumbling with generous emotion, 'with the name of your cafe, even. It shall be a shrine for artists when this story is known. Trust me faithfully to preserve for the future every smallest detail in the life and character of this great genius. Each episode has its own sacred, its precious and peculiar interest. Yes, truly, I shall mention the tamales.' "

The story is too slight to carry the burden of its irony, which is particularly striking in the broader context of its setting, the Mexican social and economic revolution, and even more so in its more limited artistic frame. It is a mere fragment of Miss Porter's knowledge of the artistic world of Mexico, and it is unfortunate that she did not complete and publish other stories on this theme since she was in Mexico during the formative stage of the artistic renaissance.

"Virgin Violeta"

"Virgin Violeta" is a more successful story, largely because Miss Porter is more concerned with the characters and because her descriptions are more vivid and her meaning more evident. The title is particularly useful in understanding the story, for, as James William Johnson has noted, her titles "almost invariably summarize symbolically the state of affairs she deals with in her story."[3]

Violeta (the color violet is emblematic of gravity and chastity), a fifteen-year-old Mexican girl of good family who had been carefully sheltered by family and by the Sisters at the convent, sat listening to her cousin Carlos and her sister Blanca read poetry. Violeta was painfully aware of her shyness and of her unattractive clothes, and jealous of her more elegantly dressed, more experienced sister. Blanca, reading the poem, " 'This torment of love which is in my heart:/I know that I suffer it, but I do not know why,' " seemed anxious to keep the lines for herself, lines which underscore Violeta's emotions; for she is tormented by love for Carlos.

In a religious picture hanging over Violeta's head, the Virgin "with enameled face set in a detached simper, forehead bald of eyebrows, extended one hand remotely over the tonsured head of the saint, who groveled in a wooden posture of ecstasy." Before his final conversion, Loyola would spend hours thinking of ways to win the favors of a lady, followed by intense periods of spiritual desires. During a vision he saw the Virgin and Son and felt loathing for all his former carnal desires and vowed never again to yield to them. Carlos stared at the picture, and Violeta noted his "furry, golden eyebrows," his beautiful mouth and chin. *Mamacita,* like a drowsy cat roused from her sleep, reminded Carlos that he must depart at a reasonable hour; and then she "relapsed into a shallow nap, as a cat rises from the rug, turns, and lies down again."

Violeta watched the two readers with "no native wisdom," for at the convent she was taught "modesty, chastity, silence, obedience" and a smattering of French, music, and arithmetic. She saw her life beginning in the future, unrolling "like a long gay carpet for her to walk upon." The carpet makes her think of a wedding, of coming from the church; but she does not visualize a bridegroom. As befits a virgin, she immediately reminds herself that she did not mean a wedding, she was thinking of a festival; she wants to read about life and love, to be free to read Carlos' poetry without hindrance, without hiding the poems in her missal.

One particular poem appealed to her schoolgirl-romantic notions, a poem about "the ghosts of nuns returning to the old square before their ruined convent, dancing in the moonlight with the shades of lovers forbidden them in life; treading with bared feet on broken glass as a penance for their loves." Violeta, dreaming of life, thought the poem was written for her, that she was one of the nuns; for her notion of love is an idealization of the sacred love of the Virgin.

She saw Carlos through tear-filled eyes, and his face appeared soft, as if he had tears on his cheeks. She felt as she often did in church, "inclosed in a cage too small."[4] Silently confessing her love for Carlos, she blushed and prayed to the Virgin. When Carlos went with her to search for his new volume of poetry, she was frightened by the sound of his walk, and stopped in the sun room, in the moonlight. His hand touched her; she saw his eyebrows hover and swoop as he kissed her. She drew away, and Carlos put his hand over her mouth to keep her from calling out. She felt intensely ill for this was not love as she had dreamed it. She threatened to tell her mother, but he insisted it was only a brotherly kiss. She felt she had made a mistake, blushed, and said "I thought—a kiss—meant—meant—." But Carlos did not help her, merely said she was young "like a little new-born calf." They returned to the others, but Violeta felt her shame, felt she had acted immodestly. The conflict in her mind over the meaning of love was preordained by her sheltered home life and by the teachings of the nuns. Carlos as worldly Loyola was not part of her immature dream.

Blanca had found the book, and Violeta's reactions demonstrate Miss Porter's great indebtedness to Joyce's *Dubliners*: "Violeta wished to cry in real earnest now. It was the last blow that Blanca should have found the book. A kiss meant nothing at all, and Carlos had walked away as if he had forgotten her. It was all mixed up with the white rivers of moonlight and the smell of warm fruit and a cold dampness on her lips that made a tiny smacking sound. She trembled and leaned over until her forehead touched *mamacita's* lap. She could not look up, ever, ever again."

Carlos, planning a trip to Paris, kissed Blanca as he was leaving; and then, as his mouth swooped to kiss Violeta, she saw only his macaw-like eyes and screamed uncontrollably. Later, *mamacita* tried to be comforting, but Violeta's world had "melted together in a confusion and misery that could not be explained, because it was all changed and uncertain." She could not read Carlos' poetry that summer, she even drew caricatures of him, and she quarreled on more equal terms with her sister. She could not settle the question which was in her mind; and, when she had to return to the convent in the fall, she wept and complained, for, she declared, there was "nothing to be learned there."

Violeta is in her sensitivity a prototype of the character of Miranda, and in her shyness she is a prototype of Elsa, the plain Swiss girl in *Ship of Fools*, who, paralyzed with fear, cannot dance with the Cuban student. The controlled images such as the furry eyebrows, the drowsing cat-like mother, the young lovers observed by the inexperienced waiting-to-be, afraid-to-be loved Violeta, the emblematic picture of the Virgin and the groveling Loyola, and the tension in the closed room are subtly intermingled.

II   *Alienation*

"Flowering Judas"

"Flowering Judas,"[5] (1930) the next Mexican story, can profit-ably be read in the light of "Where Presidents Have No Friends," Miss Porter's brilliant analysis of the Obregón revolution. Though feeling a profound respect for the aims of the movement, she sees the confusion and the cross-purposes present at both the highest and lowest levels, as further confused by foreign oppor-tunists who found support from many groups. "The result," she wrote, "is a hotbed of petty plotting, cross purposes between natives and foreigners, from the diplomats down to the un-washed grumbler who sits in the alameda and complains about the sorrows of the proletariat. In all this the men in present power are struggling toward practicable economic and political relations with the world." This story also marks a great change in Miss Porter's fictional presentation of the Mexican scene—for the first time, she presents an extended study of the expatriate in Mexico.

Miss Porter's own account of the composition of this justly famous story also provides a key to its meaning:

> "Flowering Judas" was written between seven o'clock and midnight of a very cold December, 1929, in Brooklyn. The experiences from which it was made occurred several years before, in Mexico, just after the Obregon revolution.
>
> All the characters and episodes are based on real persons and events, but naturally, as my memory worked upon them and time passed, all assumed different shapes and colors, formed gradually around a central idea, that of self-delusion, the order and meaning of the episodes changed, and became in a word fiction.
>
> The idea first came to me one evening when going to visit the girl I call Laura in the story, I passed the open window of her living room on my way to the door, through the small patio which is one of the scenes in the story. I had a brief glimpse of her sitting with an open book in her lap, but not reading, with a fixed look of pained melancholy and confusion in her face. The fat man I call Braggioni was playing the guitar and singing to her.

In that glimpse, no more than a flash, I thought I understood, or perceived, for the first time, the desperate complications of her mind and feelings, and I knew a story; perhaps not her true story, not even the real story of the whole situation, but all the same a story that seemed symbolic truth to me. If I had not seen her face at that very moment, I should never have written just this story because I should not have known it to write.[6]

Ray B. West wrote in "Katherine Anne Porter and 'Historic Memory'" that he was puzzled by the naming of the central character "because so many of the background facts concerning Laura were similar to those in Katherine Anne Porter's own experience, the strict Catholic up-bringing, the interest in modern social causes, and the fact that Miss Porter had taught in Mexico. . . ." Mr. West asked why the character was not named Miranda, and Miss Porter replied that "Laura was modeled upon a friend" with whom she taught in Mexico, but the character was a "combination of a good many people, just as was the character Braggioni. . . ." Autobiographic qualities, therefore, may be present; for she may have combined some facets of her own character and those of the fictional Miranda into the fictional Laura.

"Flowering Judas" has been a favorite story for symbol hunting, and Miss Porter has recently commented pertinently: "Symbolism happens of its own self and it comes out of something so deep in your own consciousness and your own experience that I don't think that most writers are at all conscious of their use of symbols. I never am until I see them. They come of themselves. . . . I have a great deal of religious symbolism in my stories because I have a very deep sense of religion and also I have a religious training. And I suppose you don't invent symbolism. You don't say, 'I am going to have the flowering Judas tree stand for betrayal,' but, of course, it does."[7] Miss Porter's recent statement does underline, in many ways, however, the validity of much of Ray B. West's interpretation in *The Art of Modern Fiction*. According to legend, Judas hanged himself from a redbud tree, and the title occurs in Eliot's "Gerontion":

> In the juvescence of the year
> Came Christ the tiger
> In depraved May, dogwood and chestnut, flowering judas,
> To be eaten, to be divided, to be drunk
> Among whispers.

As West points out, the Judas tree is a symbol of betrayal, and Laura's eating of the buds is a sacrament of betrayal. Braggioni, the professional revolutionary, the professional lover of men, self-pitying and ruthless, is ironically presented as a "world-saviour." Eugenio (literally the "wellborn") is somewhat Christ-like; and, like Judas, Laura is directly responsible for the death of Eugenio since she brings the narcotics he uses in his suicide.

West's analysis of the love symbols in the story is particularly influential in recent criticism of "Flowering Judas." He sees Laura incapable of participating "(1) as a divine lover in the Christian sense, for it is clear that she is incapable of divine passion when she occasionally sneaks into a small church to pray; (2) as a professional lover in the sense that Braggioni is one, for she cannot participate in the revolutionary fervor of the workers, which might be stated as an activity expressive of 'love' for their fellow men; she cannot even feel the proper emotion for the children who scribble on their blackboards, 'we lov ar titcher'; (3) as an erotic lover, for she responds for none of her three suitors, though she thoughtlessly throws one of them a rose (the symbol of erotic love). . . ."

The old man in Eliot's "Gerontion" had lost his "sight, smell, hearing, taste, and touch"; and Laura is also a wasteland figure, outside of religion, revolution, and love. Braggioni, West believes, is capable of redemption, as the foot-washing scene would indicate, but Laura is not. Therefore the theme of the story may be stated: "Only in faith and love can man live."

West, however, tends to overemphasize the religious interpretation. The wasteland-Christian symbolism is, of course, clearly present in the story, and it is used to underscore Laura's disenchantment with what she knows but cannot admit is a false revolution. Without courage to disentangle herself, she drifts along in the movement, is filled with despair, feeds on the lives of others, and realizes the full extent of her betrayal only in her symbolic dream. The dream, utilizing common Christian symbols as it does, indicates the strength of the religious and ethical system she had partially put aside while she worked in the revolutionary movement. True, she sometimes sneaked into Church, but it was to no avail, and she ended by examining the tinseled, jumbled altar with the doll-saint whose drawers, trimmed in lace, had dropped about his ankles.

The scene not only enforces the wasteland theme but also shows clearly that Laura was, by the very nature of her early social training, a false revolutionist too: she could not, for example, put aside her aristocratic preference for hand-made lace. Braggioni—the name suggests his braggart nature—has equally betrayed the revolution; but he still has some ideals, can still speak of a world order built anew after the rot of centuries had been destroyed. But he spoke of his idealism as if he were addressing followers, and he quickly promised physical violence and destruction before the new order could flourish. This obscenely fat, false revolutionist, vile as he is, is at least capable of action both revolutionary and amatory; but Laura, although she had once obviously been touched with the idealism of the movement, was now paralyzed, unable to love—even betrayed love by throwing the flower to the suitor who stood by the Judas tree.

Her involvement in Eugenio's death is clear: she allows him a final act of self-destruction. Braggioni's attitude is Am I my brother's keeper? and he has nothing but contempt for Eugenio—a fool, he calls him. Braggioni is following a completely different set of values from those of Laura, and his concern is more for the movement—and his own gratification—than with individual man. But because she has no revolutionary myths deeply implanted in her subconscious, Laura sees, in the dream, the implications of her act played out in traditional Christian terms. When Eugenio offered his body and his blood, she cried "No." Had she subconsciously been able to say "Yes" without reservations, she would have been able to continue believing in the amoral (according to Christian standards) revolution; but in crying "No," while knowing that she was, as Eugenio called her, a cannibal, she realized for the first time the extent of her betrayal of herself and of her religious, ethical, and humanitarian principles. Some of her Christian precepts were as obviously flawed—her romantic concept of self as Virgin, the hiding of her body, her fear of close human contact, her aristocratic pretenses—but she was unaware of these faults. Like a Hemingway hero, she was afraid to sleep after this dream of self-realization. Will she, frightened by her betrayal, return to her religion, a religion which in practice helped enslave the Mexicans? Will she merge Christian idealism with revolutionary idealism and find or found a more worth-while movement? Will she continue her self-isolated, wasteland existence? Miss Porter provides no answer. Laura has been a victor over self-delusion, but is not her seeming victory also ironic?

"Hacienda"

"Hacienda"[8] (1934) continues the wasteland theme of Miss Porter's work and is a story which has often been misunderstood. "Miss Porter succeeds beautifully in capturing the elusive properties of people and things," Howard Baker wrote in a review of "Hacienda," but he added what has become almost standard judgment of the work: "There is, however, an inconclusiveness in this story, a lack of a bold theme or of a sturdy fable."[9] Similarly, Elizabeth Hart in a New York *Herald Tribune Books* review of December 16, 1934, expressed disappointment in the story because it seemed mere notes for a novel; and Harry John Mooney, Jr., has complained that the narrator has no "integral function," for she "makes no comment on it, and seems to serve mainly as reporter."[10] But a reading of "Hacienda" in the light of Miss Porter's essays and stories on Mexico, the filming of Eisenstein's *Que Viva Mexico!*, and her 1940 Preface to *Flowering Judas* will answer many of the objections to what seems to be Miss Porter's least popular short novel.

The feudal quality of Mexican society contributes much of the irony in "Hacienda"; Uspensky, the Communist director, has chosen a pulque estate as the site for the filming of a movie, using as actors peons still serving in a feudal system. In actuality, Uspensky bears a close resemblance to Sergei Eisenstein, who along with his two assistants, was given a leave from the Soviet Union in 1929. After a brief, unsatisfactory stay in Hollywood, they went to Mexico to make a film. Upton Sinclair and his wife raised $25,000 for the making of *Que Viva Mexico!*

According to Marie Seton, Eisenstein's biographer, much of the actual filming took place at Tetlapaijac, a beautiful hacienda owned by Don Julio Saldwar. Eighty miles southeast of Mexico City, the main building on the estate was a fortress with "coral pink walls" and had "two high towers like sentinels rising above a sea of symmetrical, immobile grey-green cactus—the maguey...." Founded by one of Cortes' followers, the estate had remained in the hands of the Saldwar family after the revolution, Miss Seton says, "because they agreed to turn it into an agricultural cooperative. Gradually ... the peons ... were slowly approaching what might one day become a better life."[11] Miss Seton seems to have been expressing a vague hope; in Miss Porter's fictional account, at least, an army is present to prevent change.

Eisenstein originally planned to do the movie in six parts, including introduction and conclusion. Only one section, part three (Novel II—Maguey) was actually distributed commercially in the United States, and Eisenstein was not allowed to supervise the final cutting and editing of that section. Worried by mounting costs and thousands of feet of film which obviously would not be used, Upton Sinclair sent his brother-in-law Hunter Kimbrough to oversee the production. Kimbrough was, according to Miss Seton, not experienced in film-making; and he seems, because of his prudery, to have antagonized Eisenstein and his followers. Mr. Sinclair explained that his brother-in-law was "a young Southerner with very old fashioned ideals of honor" who considered Eisenstein a great artist. Mr. Sinclair added, "I doubt if he had ever heard of such a thing as a homo and he was bewildered to find himself in such company. He discovered that Eisenstein wanted money, money, money, and never had the slightest idea of keeping any promise he made. When Kimbrough obeying my orders, tried to limit the money and the subjects shot, there were furious rows."[12] The Kennerly of the novel corresponds in some respects to the picture drawn of Kimbrough in Miss Seton's book, even to having a brother-in-law who was an ardent prohibitionist, as Mr. Sinclair is.

Eisenstein's brief script for the Maguey section began with a paean to maguey, from which the Indians sucked the juice used in making pulque. "White, like milk," he characterized it— "a gift of the gods, according to legend and belief, this strongest intoxicant drowns sorrows, inflames passions. . . ." He planned to film the ancient process of pulque-making before turning to the Sebastian-Maria story: Sebastian, a peon, takes his bride, Maria, to the hacienda owner as "homage." The guards refuse to let Sebastian enter; and before the Hacendado, who is entertaining friends, can give Maria a few coins, a carriage arrives with his daughter; Maria is forgotten by all except the intoxicated villain who ravishes her. One of Sebastian's friends who sees what is happening runs to tell Sebastian, who attempts to storm the gathering but is repulsed. The distraught Sebastian lusts for revenge, organizes the peons, and makes another attempt to free Maria; but the guards are too strong and the insurgents are forced to flee. They are pursued; and the Hacendado's daughter, after killing one of the peons, is herself killed. Sebastian is finally captured and summarily executed; the section ends with Maria's finding his body among the magueys.[13]

Using as background the actual hacienda, a slightly fiction-alized version of Eisenstein's artificial plot, and the rather bizarre personalities of those gathered at the hacienda for the filming, Miss Porter transmuted these materials into fiction, using as narrator the "I," identified only as a woman writer strangely detached from the events. This disengagement is an extension of the disengagement and isolation of Laura in "Flowering Judas." In "Hacienda," the narrator who, like Heming-way's Frederick Henry, distrusts all the old shibboleths, seemingly does not attempt to get beneath the surface of the action. She is protecting herself by recording, not probing.

"Hacienda" is much more than a comedy of manners, although the narrator does delineate the foibles of the Americans, Mexicans, and Russians at the hacienda. The story begins with a brilliant scene portraying Kennerly, the business manager of the movie, in contrast to the docile Mexicans whom he regards as inferior, filthy, disease-ridden nuisances. Always in the background is the "true revolution of blessed memory" which had abolished third-class train travel, just as it had changed the names of many things "nearly always with the view to an appearance of heightened well-being for all creatures." In spite of Kennerly's outrageous Anglo-Saxon superiority, he tellingly describes the graft and corruption of the government; but he is outraged only when affected by it.

Andreyev, assistant to the famous director Uspensky, explained to the narrator, after Kennerly fell asleep, that the Russians had chosen the hacienda as a setting because the pulque-making process had not changed since the very beginning, and the hacienda itself had stayed the same. His views were borne out by the still shots from the film: the unchanged land filled with figures "under a doom imposed by the landscape," the peons filled with "instinctive suffering" but "without individual memory." The camera had caught the "ecstatic death expectancy which is in the air of Mexico." He also recounted the tangled affair after Lolita, the one professional actress in the movie, joined the film company; first she becomes the mistress of Don Gerano, then the inseparable friend of Doña Julia, Don Gerano's wife. The Doña Julia-Lolita relationship seems perverse and decadent, even in the jocularly narrated version of Andreyev.

Much of the story revolves around the various reactions to the tragedy at the hacienda that day: Justino's (the Just) shooting his sister. The Indian boy who plays one of the leads in the movie reports that Justino had shot her accidentally and that, after running away, he had been captured and returned by his friend Vicente (the Victor). One of the peons reported that this was the second time in Justino's family that a brother had killed a child. The song writer Montaña insisted the boy incestuously loved his sister:

> Ah, poor little Rosalita
> Took herself a new lover,
> Thus betraying the heart's core
> Of her impassioned brother....

But Montaña is perhaps more interested in his *corrido* than in the truth, and his theory appears no more valid than the others. Kennerly is not concerned with motives but is fearful of a damage suit brought by the parents. Later Kennerly sees the bitter irony of Justino's playing the part in the movie of a boy who by accident kills a girl (played by his sister), attempts to escape, and is captured by the character played by Vicente. He complains that the dead girl should have been photographed to add more realism to the scene in the movie. When Justino returns, he must play the scene again since the light had not been right, but Kennerly's emotions are perverted, and he thinks of this prospect with glee.

The narrator is conscious of the spirit of the grandfather, who did not understand or approve of his grandson and wife and had retired to a remote section of the hacienda "where he lived in bleak dignity and loneliness, without hope and without philosophy, perhaps contemptuous of both. . . ." His grandson lived with even less purpose: women, fast cars, airplanes. His wife led the life of a pampered aristocrat, dressed in outlandish costumes by a Hollywood designer, and carried about a foolish lap dog. Don Gerano and his wife are Mexican copies of the lost generation.

The great Uspensky is enigmatic, dressed in a monkey-suit, with a monkey face, and with "a monkey attitude towards life." He is unconcerned about the fate of Justino; Don Gerano is concerned because the judge wants a bribe to release the boy. He will not pay, because to do so would mean continual blackmail by judges. The emotions of Justino and Vicente are hidden from the narrator, but their emotions seem more intense in contrast with the insensitivity of those who at first talk endlessly of the affair but then put it out of their minds as "far away and not worth thinking about." The fate of the victimized peon rests with Velarde, "the most powerful and successful revolutionist in Mexico. He owned two pulque haciendas which had fallen to his share when the great repartition of land had taken place." Don Gerano was appealing to him, but Velarde would also demand a bribe.

The heavy, rotting smell hovering over the hacienda from the pulqueria is symbolic of the spiritual and moral corruption within the compound and of the corruption in the society itself. All over Mexico the Indians partook of the products of the hacienda: they would "swallow forgetfulness and ease by the riverful, and the money would flow silver-white into the government treasury; Don Gerano and his fellow hacendados would fret and curse, the Agrarians would raid, and ambitious politicians in the capital would be stealing right and left enough to buy such haciendas for themselves. It was all arranged." The theme of inevitability seems an echo of the passage from Ecclesiastes used by Hemingway in *The Sun Also Rises*.

When the guests visit the pulqueria, which is enveloped in

religious myths of its own, they see the figure of Maria Santisima standing in a niche, surrounded by "fly blown paper flowers" and with a perpetual light at her feet. The walls of the room were covered with a fresco telling the story of this Indian girl who discovered the divine liquor and became a half goddess. Later that day the visitors do not enter the hacienda chapel; they pose for pictures in front of the closed doors, and Montaña, the failure, plays a fat priest. The scene points out again the alienation of all those at the hacienda, except the peons.

Miss Porter skillfully interweaves the elements of the story— the satiric character sketches, the Mexican social and political scene, the tragic life of the peons, the theme of appearance-reality specially heightened by the film-making motif. The disengagement of the narrator is broken in an incident with dogs. The dogs at the hacienda kept chasing the soldiers to their accustomed place; the dogs also chased the pigs, but the pigs knew that they were not in danger and that the chase was actually a game. The narrator saw, just before arriving at the hacienda, hungry dogs chasing a rabbit, and cried out, "Run, rabbit, run!" Her Indian driver (unaware that he was symbolically a rabbit, not a dog) shouted encouragement to the dogs and offered to place a wager on the outcome. The fate of the rabbit is not given, just as Justino's fate is not known; but it is likely they both will not survive, a fate particularly meaningful in light of Miss Porter's concern for "the terrible failure of the life of man in the Western world."

"Hacienda" is not slight; it is not the mere notes for a novel. It is a brilliantly executed story of disengagement, of spiritual, physical, moral, and psychological isolation—a short novel of the lost generation. Unlike Jake Barnes and Lady Brett, who can talk about their reasons for being without hope and without faith, the narrator protects herself from the past, does not reveal the reasons for her being an observer instead of an actor, and thereby increases the totality of her isolation.

"That Tree"

"That Tree,"[14] (1934) a dramatic monologue, contains two unnamed characters—the journalist telling his story and his companion, perhaps a woman, through whose eyes we see and hear the events of the story. The journalist's monologue is interrupted only once, by a quarrel with a newspaperman.

The story is an account of the failure of a man to lead the bohemian life he dreamed of, of the falsity of that dream, of the failure of a marriage, the failure of a prim woman to enjoy life or sex—and, by implication, the failure of the Mexican social revolution. The journalist's own words turn against him, and the listener and the reader see fragmentary but sharply defined images of Mexican bohemianism, the American middle classes, American liberal magazines, American expatriates in Mexico, and the codes of conduct of the journalist, his pseudo-artistic friends, and his Indian mistress. The narration alternates between heavy irony and biting satire. The unnamed journalist had once had the romantic desire "to be a cheerful bum lying under a tree in a good climate, writing poetry," poetry he knew was worthless; but he insisted, too strongly, that he received great pleasure in composing it. His was the fatuous concept of the poet as a poverty-stricken but unshackled bum; but, after his first wife Miriam left him, he put his dream aside to become an important journalist for liberal American magazines, an authority on revolutions in Latin America. He confessed to any who would listen that Miriam's leaving him had been his making, that he had become a success just to impress her.

Miriam, even more than Laura in "Flowering Judas," was prim and proper; she took life seriously. She hated Mexicans and their culture; she held her nose when she went to the market; she refused to have an Indian servant. The squalor, the distance between expectation and reality are all painfully acute to everyone except the narrator, who could not understand why his wife cried. She hated housework; he had thought it joyful to wash the colorful pottery outside, with the heaven tree in full bloom. In the three years of their engagement, during which she saved for her dowery, she complained, much like Carol Kennicott in *Main Street,* about the dullness of the Middle West; but, once she saw her husband's bohemian friends in Mexico, she became frightened. She knew they were just waiting for their chance and would not believe his mystical explanation that the artist chose poverty. After she left him, he too finally decided his own notions on art and artists were romantic.

He put aside part of his bohemian life to "walk the chalk line" with Miriam. Their chalk lines were different; she had violated his code of conduct when four generals, just after the Obregón Revolution, came to the city for the installation of the new government. "They infested the steam baths, where they took off their soiled campaign harness and sweated away the fumes of tequila and fornication, and they infested the cafés to get drunk again on champagne, and pick up the French whores who had been imported for the festivities of the presidential inauguration." When the generals, quarreling among themselves, reached for their pistols, all the Mexican girls on the dance floor swung their escorts, to act as shields (the room was "frozen," the music stopped); but Miriam had hidden under a table. She could never understand why he was humiliated by her breaking a Hemingwayish code. He broke his own code of conduct when he argued with the newspaperman, but he was too self-centered to be aware of this.

At times, as the drink pushed aside his defenses, the journalist saw some of the truth about himself, saw that his concept of the artist was romantic; but he could draw no conclusions except those of Miriam and the middle classes: success had to be tangible, monetarily rewarding, and socially elevating.

Miriam had won. Two wives later, he was taking her back, as mistress, he claimed; but his companion knew better. He thought Miriam would now walk a chalk line—he drew a symbolic line on the table cloth, then crosshatched it—but it was he, his companion knows, who would follow the line. The listener wanted to say, "Don't forget to invite me to your wedding," but did not. More deluded than Miranda at the end of "Old Mortality," the journalist said to "the shadow opposite"—an image which continues the wasteland theme of earlier Mexican stories—as they sat in the café now almost emptied, the orchestra leaving: "I suppose you think I don't know—"; then he paused for effect, "I don't know what's happening, this time," he said, "don't deceive yourself. This time, I know." He admonished himself, as before a mirror. As in "My Last Duchess," we have seen clearly the character of a self-deluded, success-failure of a man.

Mooney, in his pamphlet on Miss Porter, rather misses the point when he complains that we do not care about the journalist.

Miss Porter has used the story of the journalist as a way of dissecting several fragments of American and Mexican culture. The hollowness, the trickery, the chicanery—all are expertly, mercilessly exposed.

From almost complete immersion in Mexican culture in "María Concepción," Miss Porter's artistic attitude toward her Mexican materials changed drastically over the years. Although her essays on Mexico presented frankly the artistic, political, and economic changes in Mexico after the revolution, and she did not accept all the changes naïvely, she at first had great expectations for the country. Forty years later, Miss Porter tried to explain her changed view of the world and of Mexico. She felt that the evil which she described in *Ship of Fools* "Wouldn't have happened if any of the people opposed to it had taken hold and not let it happen." In Mexico she had seen "clowns like Hitler" and she realized, on her voyage to Europe in 1931, that "the tragedy of our times is not an accident but a total accident." She considered the voyage "a godsent experience, and yet I wouldn't have been able to see any of these things in perspective if I hadn't first seen them in Mexico. But in Mexico there was always something good about it. In Mexico there was always some *chance* of salvation."[15]

Miss Porter's later fiction about Mexico, beginning with "Flowering Judas," does not, however, always demonstrate this "*chance* of salvation," for she turned from the theme of Mexicans in Mexican culture (though, admittedly, she does not idealize the Mexicans in her early stories) to the expatriate, disenchanted, often disengaged American in Mexico. Thus the movement in the fiction was from inside the Mexican culture to disengagement from it. In the first chapter of *Ship of Fools*, Mexico is treated with great disgust and revulsion. The opening sentence sets the tone for what is to follow: "The port town of Veracruz is a little purgatory between land and sea for the traveler, but the people who live there are very fond of themselves and the town they have helped to make." The "*chance* of salvation" is not clearly evident.

CHAPTER 3

The Native Land of My Heart

D URING the 1920's and early 1930's, Miss Porter lived in Mexico, Bermuda, Spain, Germany, Switzerland, and France. When she wrote " 'Noon Wine': The Sources" in 1956, she confessed that those places were "right" and "timely" for her then but that she had not felt at home. All the time, she made notes on stories about Central Texas, her part of the South. "I was," she says, "almost instinctively living in a sustained state of mind and feeling, quietly and secretly, comparing one thing with another, always remembering and remembering; and all sorts of things were falling into their proper places, taking on their natural shapes and sizes, and going back and back clearly into right perspective—right for me as an artist, I simply mean to say; and it was like breathing—I did not have consciously to urge myself to think about it." These years, spent in what she has elsewhere called a "constant exercise of memory," gave the past back to her; and this exploration of what had been closely parallels the experience of other expatriates of the 1920's and 1930's who were returning to their native land for subjects to treat in their art.

In an evocative passage from " 'Noon Wine': the Sources" she has tried to capture part of her past:

"This summer country of my childhood, this place of memory, is filled with landscapes shimmering in light and color, moving with sounds and shapes I hardly ever describe, or put in my stories in so many words; they form only the living background of what I am trying to tell, so familiar to my characters they would hardly notice them; the sound of mourning doves in the live oaks, the childish voices of parrots chattering on every back porch in the little towns, the hoverings of buzzards in the high blue air—all the life of that soft blackland farming country. . . . The colors and tastes all had their smells, as the sounds have now their echoes: the bitter whiff of air over a sprawl of animal skeleton after the buzzards were gone; the smells and flavors of roses and melons, . . . and the sickly sweetness of chinaberry florets; . . . the delicious milky green corn, the savory hot corn bread eaten with still-warm sweet milk. . . ."

This poetic passage is reminiscent of Mark Twain's recollection of the Quarles Farm in his *Autobiography;* the Southern scene, the smells, the foods are much the same. Miss Porter, just as Mark Twain did, has avoided an Edenic description, for she has buzzards and the cloying, sickly-sweet subtropical smells everpresent in her "shimmering landscape."

Social structure in Miss Porter's childhood was clearly defined. Uncle Jimbilly, one of the ex-slaves, knew all of his rights and privileges; but he could claim them only as long as he performed his assigned duties. The older generation—those who were products of the South before the Civil War—still ruled, even though the war had ended thirty years before. They acted, Miss Porter says, "as if the final word had gone out long ago on manners, morality, religion, even politics: nothing was ever to change, they said, and even as they spoke, everything was changing, shifting, disappearing." The changes had been going on rapidly since the war, but they still insisted that they were living in a society based on traditional Christian beliefs. These beliefs were primarily Protestant but not puritanical, for they could, as the fundamentalists could not, see the difference between wine-drinking and adultery.

In "Portrait: Old South" Miss Porter provides a charming account of her grandparents and the vanished past. They had been married in Kentucky about 1850, in a great family ceremony. One of the flower girls, decades later, wrote Miss Porter about the wedding; the ancient lady remembered the great silver candlesticks, the huge cake, the butter dish which held at least ten pounds of butter molded into a floral design, the tremendous wedding dinner. The flower girl lived to boast of the feast; but she, and the others who lived another decade, were destined to eat corn bread.

The Porter family fortunes were depleted by the war, and Miss Porter thinks "the evil turn of fortune" in the grandmother's life made her "truly heroic." Mrs. Porter had no such romantic notions about herself; she even considered her poverty as temporary, and as long as she lived the family never really faced its problems.

Mrs. Porter had expected hordes of servants to look after her eleven children, for her nature was social. But, her grand-daughter wrote, she entertained lavishly with remnants of her finery, spoiled her children and her grandchildren, punishing them erratically and ineffectually. Nor was she willfully eccentric; her horseback riding until the year of her death and her enjoyment of cubeb cigarettes and Bourbon seemed natural. This figure of the grandmother was the most important influence in Miss Porter's life, and in the Miranda stories the grandmother takes on mythic qualities. Her name Sophia Jane Rhea indicates much of this attitude, for Sophia means skill, intelligence, or wisdom; Jane is a feminine form of John which means literally, the Lord is gracious; and Rhea was the mother of the Gods.

I *Grandmother and Southern Society*

"The Source"

"The Source"[1] is an introduction to the grandmother and her family and to Southern society. Along with "The Witness," "The Old Order," and "The Last Leaf," "The Source" provides a fascinating but fragmentary account of the world of Sophia Jane Rhea, which was to help mold the character of Miranda— just as Catherine Anne Porter and Southern society were important in forming Katherine Anne Porter, both as person and artist.

Early every summer, before the three grandchildren were sent from the town house to the farm, the grandmother began to think of life at the farm, began to talk of the change and relaxation soon to be hers, though in fact the change meant great physical exertion and even tighter control over family affairs. Harry, widowed father of the children, took on an air of patience, masking his "annoyance at the coming upsets and inconveniences to be endured at the farm"; but she represented an authority which could not be challenged.

Although she knew perfectly well she would be a slave driver at the farm, she imagined herself walking through the orchard, pruning the rose bushes, training the honeysuckle; and just for such occasions she took with her a large shepherdess hat which had been woven just after the Civil War, a symbol of the past and of what she would like to have been. But she never wore the hat, never gave way to her romantic dreams. Instead, she put on a stiffly starched bonnet, with starch-stiffened, long strings—a visual symbol of her unbending nature.

She had suffered greatly in her times, and the brutal past came flooding in to her every year when the peach tree bloomed outside the town house: she had planted five orchards in three states but now could see only one tree blooming. The peach tree outwardly represented "all her beloved trees still blooming, flourishing, and preparing to bring forth fruit in their separate places." The passage gains in intensity because the reader instinctively thinks of Chekhov's *The Cherry Orchard*.

When she arrived at the farm, accompanied by the other members of the family, Hinry (certainly pronounced and perhaps spelled this way) noticed only the grandmother, showing his respect for the source of power at the farm. She thought of her return as a coming home to the land, to the people, and immediately set out, still wearing her widow's bonnet, to inspect the house, the Negro quarters, gardens, barns, fields. At the Negro quarters, she would be told—as she poked into their belongings, ordering everything to be whitewashed, or varnished, or washed—that things were in disorder because of outside work, because of the miserliness of the overseer hired hand. Obviously, she regarded them and treated them just as she had when they were slaves and soothed petty or major annoyances; but she did not consider making any basic changes in the life of the Negro.

Once she turned to the main house, she dusted the sets of Dickens, Scott, Thackeray, Dante, Pope, Milton, and Dr. Johnson's Dictionary—her tastes were standard (did not include American or contemporary authors) and conservative, as her preference for Dr. Johnson's monumental but by then outdated dictionary demonstrates. (Miss Porter has confirmed that these were the reading tastes of Mrs. Porter.) The whole house was in turmoil, rugs being dusted, curtains washed, kitchen straightened; and for two weeks she reorganized the whole farm.

The children had mixed feelings about her; she had been a fixed reality for them since their own mother had died young and she had taken them over, but they also recognized her as a tyrant. No matter how much they loved her, they were pleased when she started making preparations to return to the town house. Miranda does not emerge as a character to evaluate the grandmother, and the children's reaction is a collective one.

Signaling the close of her visit, she went through the ritual of riding Fiddler again—not the original Fiddler, we learn in "The Old Order," but the last in a long line going back to her fifth year. She rode Fiddler as a sign of her strength. Fiddler was old, too, and stiff; and she could see the signs of his age, but she did not admit her own age and infirmities. Then she would take a stroll in the orchard, still not wearing her shepherdess hat, to make final improvements here and there, missing nothing.

Realizing that the town house was by now in a state of disorder, she would leave the farm to restore it again. Her greatest delight was in imposing what was essentially an unnatural order. The cycle never ended: disorder to be ordered, but disorder not to be conquered, always multiplying.

Taken alone, the story is a remarkable portrait of a strong-willed Southern aristocrat. Seen as the introduction to the Miranda stories, it is even more effective, for one sees the source of the grandmother's power and control over family and farm and that the grandmother is herself the source of the strengths and weaknesses of the whole Rhea family.

"The Witness"

The grandmother had many connections with the past, including Fiddler, the shepherdess hat, her lost orchards; but the children had another glimpse—though limited—of the past through Uncle Jimbilly, formerly a family slave. In "The Witness"[2] we learn that he did odd jobs about the farm, but was no Uncle Remus, although he would, if asked correctly, carve tombstones to be placed on the graves of the dead birds and animals buried by the children. They went through elaborate ceremonies, no doubt because of their ever-present, yet uncomprehending, awareness of the death of both humans and animals. While Uncle Jimbilly carved the marker, he told long ghost stories which they didn't understand—had he seen the ghost? was it a ghost or a man? His narrative technique seems similar to James's in "The Turn of the Screw," but generally he talked of the brutalities inflicted upon the Negro in slave times, though he was not tortured because he belonged to Sophia Jane.

"Dey used to take 'em out and tie 'em down and whup 'em," he would mutter, "wid gret big leather strops inch thick long as yo' ahm, wid round holes ... in 'em so's evey time dey hit 'em de hide and de meat done come off dey bones in little round chunks." Then he would say, they put corn shucks on their backs, set them afire, and then poured vinegar over the staunched wounds. The children—Maria, ten; Paul, eight; and Miranda, six—could not quite believe his accounts of slavery, but the stories made them nervous. They were hearing a mythic, violent presentation of the life of a Southern Negro, were getting a glimpse of slavery both distorted and accurate. The accounts of slavery which they heard from the elders collided with the stories by Uncle Jimbilly. Which should they accept, which reject? Uncle Jimbilly was cantankerous and religious— no, he would not carve "Safe in Heaven" as an epitaph for a tame jackrabbit—but he lacked authority, not because he was a Negro, but because he adopted a role which the children could see through. Exasperated with the children, he would threaten to skin them alive, to pull their teeth to make a new set for the tramp, Old Man Ronk; but he never got around to doing any of these things. His threats of violence were obvious, exaggerated, and even the "most credulous child" was not frightened by them.

The children in this story are given names, and their characters begin to emerge: Maria is prissy; Paul is sad-looking; and Miranda is "quick" and "flighty." Again, this story takes on meaning in the context of all the Miranda stories. More importantly, the children are learning to evaluate the testimony of a witness to the past, a witness whose testimony runs counter to the Southern and the family myths about that past.

"The Old Order"

"The Old Order"[3] sketches in the whole life span of the grandmother and ends with her death and the impending new order. Moving back and forth in time, the story begins with her last years, when she sat with the ex-slave Nannie, talking endlessly about the past, institutionalizing and protecting it. The attitude of the children is clearly stated: they were faintly embarrassed by their grandmother's old-fashioned ways. The two old ladies, their lives intertwined since Sophia Jane was five—Nannie's age and birthdate were unknown, but Sophia Jane had provided her with each—sat with the scraps of past finery, making patchwork coverings for such things as a functional rolling pin hewn by a famous pioneer ancestor. As they sewed, they covered the past with the finery of their talk. Even the future seemed a repetition of their past: "They would agree that nothing remained of life as they had known it, the world was changing swiftly, but by the mysterious logic of hope they insisted that each change was probably the last; or if not, a series of changes might bring them, blessedly, back full-circle to the old ways they had known." Actually, the past had been bitter for them both; the grandmother had attempted, as an authoritarian figure, to keep her world stable; Nannie had been assigned a place in the world and had always obeyed.

Sophia Jane's father had bought Nannie and her parents in 1832 (Mrs. Porter was born in 1827 and would have been five in 1832). The father bought Sophia Jane a pony, the original Fiddler, at the same time; but she demanded the little pot-bellied Nannie, seemingly so worthless that she had been sold for $20 by a family emigrating to Texas. The sale, the crowds, the events of the auction seemed, decades later, almost mythic to Nannie; but she was horrified, when at the wedding of one of the grandmother's granddaughters to a grandson of Nannie's original owner, that the old gentleman mentioned to Nannie her low price. Emancipated, Nannie still measured her worth, at least partially, by the monetary standards of slavery.

The grandmother, married to her cousin Stephen, a weak man, a dissipator of her fortune, was contemptuous of men. After the death of her husband, she moved the family to Louisiana to take over a sugar refinery, but saw that she could not manage it. She then sold it at a loss to move to the Central-Texas land her husband had bought years before. Since Mr. Porter died in 1879, these events cannot be strictly true; for artistic reasons Miss Porter seems to have emphasized the matriarchal aspects of the family.

Her feelings were the important ones and not to be tampered with; her opinions were always correct. Her children grew up and married; she helped them establish homes, but they fled her domination. She found faults everywhere: Miranda's mother had been too delicate, a failure as a housekeeper, and could not bear children successfully.

Just as she was beginning to work on the faults of the orphaned children, she died. Characteristically, she was trying to set disorder aright, or rather what she deemed disorder, in the household of a son and daughter-in-law when she died. Completely ignoring the wishes of the young Mrs. Porter, the grandmother was reorganizing the garden, which called for moving a fifty-foot adobe wall; she announced how well she felt, and fell dead. With her death, we learn in other Miranda stories, the family began to come apart even more rapidly, for the grandmother's power in the family was both actual and mythic. The family's strongest connections with the dead weight of the past were severed, and it now had no real directions to follow. The extent of the change is explored briefly but poetically in "The Last Leaf."

"The Last Leaf"

"The Last Leaf"[4] is a fitting close to the first section of the family chronicle, for after Sophia Jane's death, Nannie, old and decrepit herself, surprised the family by moving away from the family house to a small cabin, a cabin which was symbolically across the creek. The children had tried to assure the old woman that they loved her, but she really did not care; her ties were with the past, and she was now ready for her own death. The world of the Rhea family was changing: "the old world was sliding from under their feet, they had not yet laid hold of the new one." The disillusionment and decay were similar to that in Prospero's speech in *The Tempest*:

> These our actors,
> As I foretold you, were all spirits, and
> Are melted into air, into thin air;
> And, like the baseless fabric of this vision,
> The cloud-capp'd towers, the gorgeous palaces,
> The solemn temples, the great globe itself,
> Yea, all which it inherit, shall dissolve
> And, like this insubstantial pageant faded
> Leave not a rack behind. We are such stuff
> As dreams are made on, and our little life
> Is rounded with a sleep (IV. i. 148-58).

The family needed Nannie as servant and matriarchal figure. She would return to them briefly, accept their gifts (offered as bribes that she might return permanently); but, with her new independence, she always returned to her own cabin. Uncle Jimbilly, her husband of convenience, tried to return to her; but she would not, she said, spend the rest of her life waiting on him: "I've served my time, I've done my do, and dat's all." In rejecting the present, she returned, not to her past with grandmother Rhea, but to an African tribal past; she is repeatedly described in terms of African nobility.

She was to the Rheas a tie to their own past, and she managed to control Harry by insisting she had suckled him (in "The Old Order" we learn that Nanny had been a wet nurse for the elder Rhea children, but not to Harry). While Nannie's facts were not literally true, he always gave in to "the smothering matriarchal tyranny to which he had been delivered by the death of his father. Still he submitted, being of the latest generation of sons who acknowledged, however reluctantly, however bitterly, their mystical never to be forgiven debt to the womb that bore them, and the breast that suckled them." In this brief passage, the essential weakness of Harry is subtly probed; like his father, Harry allowed women to dominate.

Nannie's control, since she was the last leaf, was not to last. She does, however, through Miss Porter's story, take on permanence, just as the leaf in O. Henry's story lasted because it was painted on the wall. Miss Porter avoided the trick ending of her distant kinsman, just as she avoided the easy moral of Oliver Wendell Holmes's poem:

> And if I should live to be
> The last leaf upon the tree
>   In the spring,
> Let them smile, as I do now,
> At the old forsaken bough
>   Where I cling.

II *Miranda the Child*

The stories which follow are arranged in approximate chronological order, not in the order of their composition, to allow a clearer presentation of Miranda's discovery of and initiation into the world. These stories, among Miss Porter's finest, are complex, subtle probings by the sensitive Miranda in trying to find her way in a world far different from the seemingly stable universe of Grandmother Rhea.

"The Fig Tree"

> Jesus saw Nathanael coming to him, and saith of him, Behold an Israelite indeed, in whom is no guile!
>
> Nathanael saith unto him, Whence knowest thou me? Jesus answered and said unto him, Before that Philip called thee, when thou wast under the fig tree, I saw thee.
>
> Nathanael answered and saith unto him, Rabbi, thou art the Son of God; thou art the King of Israel.
>
> Jesus answered and said unto him, Because I said unto thee, I saw thee under the fig tree, believest thou? thou shalt see greater things than these.
>
> And he saith unto him, Verily, verily, I say unto you, Hereafter ye shall see heaven open, and the angels of God ascending and descending upon the Son of man (John 1: 47-51).

"The Fig Tree"[5] concentrates on the character of Miranda, but always a Miranda with a particular, tangible past, a Miranda who is product of the Lost Cause and its aftermath; and always implicit is the knowledge that she is a granddaughter of Sophia Jane. Miss Porter's Miranda, as Edward Greenfield Schwartz pointed out in "The Fictions of Memory," begins her journey where Shakespeare's heroine ends hers. Shakespeare's Miranda cried out

> O, wonder!
> How many goodly creatures are there here!
> How beauteous mankind is! O brave new world
> That has such people in't (V. i. 181-84).

She was too sheltered to know that her belief in beauty and nobility was largely deceptive, and she had too little experience to understand Prospero's answer, " 'Tis new to thee." Shakespeare used the name Miranda in the Latin sense of strange and wonderful, but Miss Porter has added to this the Spanish meaning—"the seeing one"; for Miranda in the later stories has the ability to see through the shams of her society and her training. In "The Fig Tree" she sees her grandmother and Aunt Eliza clearly, realizing, because of her watchfulness, many of the absurdities of the adult world. Miranda as "seeing one" is particularly evident because it is Miranda, disguised in third person, telling the story of the grandmother, telling all the Miranda stories. At times the narrator ranges through time, employing a distance which allows great perspective; in other stories, including "The Fig Tree," the point of view, the emotions, the vocabulary, are that of the child.

"The Fig Tree," written in Paris in 1934, was to have been included in *The Leaning Tower* collection but was lost, finally rediscovered, and published in *Harper's Magazine* in June, 1960. The note about it in *Harper's* refers to it "as the last of the Miranda stories"; and, if this be true, the fabled forty stories still on Miss Porter's desk are not part of the Miranda cycle, and the account of Miranda and the Rheas is now as complete as Miss Porter intends to make it. (Miss Porter in the July 28, 1961, issue of *Time* is quoted as saying, "I would like to write about two wonderful old slaves who were my grandmother's companions, but someone is always giving a low name to good things and I suppose the N.A.A.C.P. would say I was glorifying Uncle Tomism." The element of Uncle Tomism is completely absent in stories about Uncle Jimbilly and Aunt Nannie, and it may well be that Miss Porter is planning stories about these two important characters in Miranda's past.)

"The Fig Tree" has as its literary background Blake's *Songs of Innocence* and *Songs of Experience*. Miss Porter goes far beyond the chimney-sweep poems with their dramatic use of "'weep! 'weep!,"[6] key words in "The Fig Tree," but she appears to be deeply indebted to Blake's imaginary world. It is characteristic of Miss Porter, however, that the borrowings are completely integrated into her own special fictional world and are not extraneous quotations nor paradings of erudite knowledge.

"The Chimney Sweeper" poem in *Songs of Innocence* begins with an explanation—the sweeper's mother had died when he was young, and his father had sold him when he could barely say "'weep!" He consoled his companion Tom, whose curly white hair had been clipped, saying that the soot would not now spoil the hair. That night, Tom dreamed of thousands of sweepers locked in "coffins of black" released by an Angel, running across the green plain, washing in the river, and finally ascending. The Angel told Tom that if he were good, God would be his father and he would never be without joy. When Tom awoke, happy at these prospects of future happiness, he believed, "So if all do their duty they need not fear harm."

In *Songs of Experience*, however, the chimney sweeper cries "'weep!" while his parents are in church. Because he had been happy on the heath, his parents had put him into "the clothes of death" and taught him to sing "the notes of woe." He concluded,

> And because I am happy & dance & sing,
> They think they have done me no injury,
> And are gone to praise God & His Priest & King
> Who make up a heaven of our misery.

From the beginning of Miss Porter's story, Miranda is shown between the state of innocence and experience. She is first shown struggling with Aunt Nannie who was combing her hair. Aunt Nannie, following the order of Harry, drew the hair back and put a band around it, an act similar to the cutting of Tom's hair. Nannie firmly attached a bonnet which the father was insisting that Miranda wear; Miranda's face was not to be spoiled with freckles. Grandmother, Harry, and Nannie, all restricted Miranda's innocent joys, by their very acts pushing her toward knowledge but at the same time attempting to keep her pure—keep her skin from being blemished. The restrictions of the elders were essentially the same as those of the parents in the "Chimney Sweeper" poem in *Songs of Experience*.

The summer day the family was to leave for the family farm named Cedar Grove, but which Harry called Halifax because it was hot there, Miranda began asking if the family was going to Halifax. Unaware of the slang meaning of the word, Miranda was admonished by Grandmother Rhea to call things by their right names, but Miranda noticed that Harry did not call the grandmother by her correct name: she was not *mammy* or *mama*. These thoughts led to thoughts of death:

"Mama was dead. Dead meant gone away forever. Dying was something that happened all the time, to people and everything else. Somebody died, and there was a long string of carriages going at a slow walk over the rocky ridge of the hill toward the river while the bell tolled and tolled, and that person was never seen again by anybody." This scene, which is also archetypal, is an accurate reproduction of the Indian Creek landscape, except that the funeral procession for Mrs. Porter would have gone from the house on the river, across the rolling hills, to the church, and then to the cemetery. Miranda's literal concept of death, her acceptance of its naturalness, stems from her acceptance of the cycle of birth and death in both animals and man. But to her natural feelings are added the rituals of death she has learned from the death of her own mother and of neighbors and relatives.

After Miranda found the dead chicken in the fig grove, she immediately began the adult-learned ritual of burial, selecting the shoe box of right size and attempting to make the partially grown chicken as attractive as possible. The fig has several connotations in the story in addition to Jesus' statement to Nathanael. After Adam and Eve fell from their state of innocence, they covered themselves with aprons of fig leaves; the fig grove was a dark and shady place, and in many mythologies groves or dark forests are often connected with evil; and the fig is also sometimes a fertility symbol.

Miranda had to hurry with her preparations for the burial, for had she been discovered in getting the box she would have had to explain; and, by the time the explanation was finished and permission granted, the spontaneity, the joy would have vanished. Just after she had made a mound over the grave, a mound just like the one on human graves, she heard a strange sound, "weep, weep, weep." In her state of innocence she had made no distinction in animal and human life, and she had afforded the chicken a child-like version of a Southern, Christian burial. The sound "weep" at first made her think she had buried the chick alive, although she knew perfectly well how to tell when all kinds of animals were dead.

Foiled from digging into the grave to see if the chicken were dead, for the Rhea party was ready to leave for Halifax, Miranda began to cry but could not, would not explain why she was crying. The adults were, as usual, uncomprehending (Grandmother Rhea could not even tell the difference between town and Halifax figs), and the father thought Miranda was having a tantrum because she had left a doll behind. He had not discovered that Miranda was not interested in inanimate things; she loved live things (doll clothes were fun to put on kittens who tore them off). It was the promise of forty kittens at Cedar Grove (Harry called it by its proper name) that finally calmed Miranda; as in "María Concepción," life was triumphing over death.

At Cedar Grove, they joined Great-Aunt Eliza, amateur scientist, who with Hinry as assistant put up her telescope on the hen house. Dressed in snuff-colored clothes, with snuff-colored eyes, iron-gray hair looking like a wig, Eliza—gathering specimens, wielding both telescope and microscope, quarreling with Sophia Jane—is a remarkably complex and comic figure. She was perhaps named for Eliza in Joyce's "Two Sisters" though the snuff-taking is transferred from Father Flynn. Miranda's reactions toward her are again colored by both innocence and experience. Miranda accepted her as a part of the Halifax world, but she rejected the snuff-flavored gumdrop by washing it and the smell away (a parallel to the boy's refusal of biscuit in "The Sisters"), and she learned more about the adult world when she saw Eliza and Sophia Jane bickering. Like Shakespeare's Miranda, Miss Porter's character watched and listened carefully "for everything in the world was strange to her and something she had to know about." She saw that the two old women were proud of having children and grandchildren, and that they knew exactly what children were to do in every situation. When Miranda saw them arguing just as she and Maria did, she became "a little frightened" and began to move away. She also learned that the grandmother's strict social standards were not always as stringent as they appeared, for Sophia Jane spoke of snuff-dipping as a low-class habit but ignored her own sister's addiction to snuff.

Although the children were not allowed to play at the table, Eliza brought her scientific specimens to dinner and told Sophia Jane, who asked what she was doing, that she wouldn't know if told. Eliza's approach to science was religious: she sat over her experiments "as if she were saying her prayers." Her action, then, closely parallels that of the church-going parents in Blake's poem.

The night Eliza allowed the children to gaze at the stars, she had to admit that science did not have all the answers. Miranda, upon seeing the moon, cried out, "Oh, it's like another world!" But, when she wanted to know if the millions of other worlds were the same as earth, Eliza replied, "Nobody knows, child ..." and Miranda sang "nobody knows" in her head, dazzled with joy, still in a state of innocence, still accepting the mysteries.

Returning to the house through the dewy path which ran through the fig grove, Miranda could smell the leaves and reached up for luck and touched one. When she heard the "weep" sound again, she cried out; and Eliza explained in uncomplicated scientific terms that the sound came from the tree frogs which, she said, shed their skins by pulling them over their heads as if they were shirts and then ate them. She is thus offering a substitute mystery, but her accuracy is in question, since she said the frogs were the first of the season; if the sound came from frogs, Miranda had heard them earlier in the other fig grove.

Miranda trusted the answer: " 'Thank you, Ma'am,' Miranda remembered finally to say through her fog of bliss at hearing the tree frogs sing, Weep weep...." But, one can properly ask, will the scientific answer be enough for Miranda? It has allayed one fear, but it has not explained the mysteries of life and death. She has accepted an explanation which was, in fact, based on a single vision of life. Even the narrator distrusts the implicit trust of Miranda, for Miranda is described as in a fog of bliss. The mist perhaps hides other questions, other answers. Miranda in "Pale Horse, Pale Rider," like Nathanael, is to see "heaven open."

"The Circus"

The young Miranda, in "The Circus,"[7] is seen along with her family and visiting relatives, a motley lot, already inside an enormous circus tent, a microcosm of the world. At first Miranda felt comfortable; she wanted to grow up to be just like Cousin Miranda, surrounded by suitors. Looking down under the plank seats, Miranda saw little ruffians staring up at her.

(The scene is the forerunner of the passages in *Ship of Fools* in which the first-class passengers peer down at inmates in steerage.) One whispered and nudged another; and, when Miranda asked Dicey what they were doing, Dicey looked, drew her knees together, and warned Miranda to "stop throwin' yo' legs around that way."

Miranda was unaware of the sexual meaning of the reply, but her initiation into the horrors of the world came immediately. The blaring band, the smells, the colors were too much for the little girl; and she cried out in panic and closed her eyes against the scene. Laughter from the audience made her open her eyes; but the mirth was deceptive, for the audience was amused by a clown with a whitened face, tufted eyebrows, and scarlet mouth painted in perpetual grimace. At first, Miranda thought he was walking on air or flying; but, when she saw he was walking on a thin wire, she was terrified.[8] The crowd was delighted by his feigned falls, with his comic flirtations with death, as he clung to the wire with one leg, the other waving about like a feeler. (Charles Kaplan has pertinently observed that animal and insect imagery is used to describe humans in this story and human images used to describe animals.) The sensitive Miranda could not bear the audience's shrieking and laughing "like devils in delicious torment." She screamed and cried and was sent home with Dicey. Grandmother Rhea disapproved of circuses and sat watching with her veil only half raised.

As Miranda was being carried out, she saw at the exit a dwarf dressed as a gnome; he stared at her with inhuman eyes (he is an early study of Herr Glocken in *Ship of Fools*), and Miranda struck at him. Before Dicey could get her away, Miranda saw the look of displeasure which she was much accustomed to and was newly afraid because she knew he was human. She had seen within the circus tent obscene sexual leers, craven pandering to the audience's desire for mordant humor in the parody of life-death being played out on the wire, and adult disapproval in the eyes of the misshapen dwarf.

The displeasure and disgust of the dwarf were to be repeated all the rest of the day: Dicey grumbled all the way home, careful not to go too far, for she was a Negro servant and understood perfectly her limited freedom. When the family returned, the other children described the circus in detail, sympathized with Dicey, and looked accusingly at Miranda, with malice in their eyes as they tormented her. Harry, knowing his mother's dislike of circuses, remarked that no harm had been done, but Grandmother Rhea, echoing Blake, said: "The fruits of their present are in a future so far off, neither of us may live to know whether harm has been done or not. That is the trouble." She could understand partially the reactions of the child, but she could not communicate with her, could not ease her pain. The father, still uncomprehending, even asked Miranda what good it had done her to miss the circus.

The question made Miranda cry again, and she and her supper were sent to her room. Miranda tried to imagine that the circus was what the other children thought it, bright and colorful and fun; but, when she fell asleep, all of her inventions fled, and she saw the terrified face of the clown falling to his death and the grimace of the dwarf. She screamed in her sleep, tried to scream away the torments she had seen that day. Dicey threatened to spank her, and Miranda, who usually announced that she minded only her grandmother, was too afraid to talk back to Dicey. Generally she did not mind what adults felt about her, but in her fear, she begged Dicey not to be angry, to stay on with her, and (like Hemingway's Jake Barnes) to leave the light on.

Dicey, collecting her Christian charity, controlled her exasperation and tried to soothe the child. Her message, outwardly calming as it was, was as false and deceptive as the scenes Miranda had seen at the circus: "Now you jes shut yo eyes and go to sleep. I ain't going to leave you. Dicey ain't mad at nobody ... nobody in the whole worl'...." Miss Porter captures in this brief story much of the horror and destruction which she later deals with in *Ship of Fools*.

"The Grave"

The action of "The Grave"[9] is set in a frame important for the understanding of the story. The first paragraph deals, in a restricted way, with the family history, compressing much of our knowledge of the Rheas into comments about the many moves of the grandfather's body. Grandmother Rhea of the fictional account had moved the body first to Louisiana and then to the family burial ground on the farm; but the family tomb in Kyle indicates that the grandfather died in 1879, seemingly after the Porters moved to Texas. As the story opens in 1903, the body is being moved to the public cemetery. The last paragraph, recounting a scene almost twenty years later, comments on and extends the significance of the event.

The two scenes within the frame are seemingly simple. The children Paul and Miranda, on their way hunting, play in the empty grave of their grandfather; Paul found there a ring and Miranda a dove-shaped screw head from the coffin. After leaving the burial ground, Paul shot a rabbit about to give birth; and for the first time Miranda understood the process of birth. The limited point of view—sometimes swooping close to Miranda, entering into her mind, recording her feelings and emotions; at other times withdrawing, increasing the air of objectivity; and sometimes shifting to the point of view of Paul, thereby portraying him in more depth and also giving the reader another view of Miranda—is particularly skillful.

In a blinding hot sun that day as the two children were hunting, they entered the burial ground and were awed when they saw the graves. At the age of nine, Miranda was still largely innocent, . seemingly little influenced by the terrible discoveries she had made earlier in "The Fig Tree" and in "The Circus." With the coffin gone, the grave was merely a hole in the ground; and she leaped into it, scratching about as if she were a young animal. The earth had a pleasant, corrupt smell, and she found a silver dove with a deep cleft in the breast; the grandfather's body had found no peace, and the children, after finding the flawed symbol of peace and innocence, went on with their hunting expedition. The ring Paul found in the corrupt earth was a gold band, probably a wedding ring, engraved with flowers and leaves, fertility symbols. They traded, and Miranda wore the ring on her thumb, literally because she was young and it fit there, but symbolically because she was not then ready to wear such a band on the correct finger.

They then fled the cemetery, for the land was no longer theirs, and they were afraid of being called trespassers. They continued their hunting expedition; although Paul had given elaborate instructions, Miranda's reactions were feminine when she saw a bird or rabbit, and she almost never hit anything. They squabbled about their shooting rights; Paul claimed the right to shoot first if they saw a rabbit or dove, and Miranda asked idly if she could fire first if they saw a snake.

Immediately after this unconscious Eve-slaying-evil and Freudian sexual image, Miranda lost interest in shooting; she became interested in the gold ring on her thumb. She was then dressed asexually in hired-man's hat, thick sandals, and overalls, the wearing apparel she preferred, since she had not yet had any feminine stirrings and since her father did not object—it saved her dresses for school. But the ring made her want to return to the house, bathe, dust herself with violet talcum powder, and put on her most feminine dress. Actually, this was not all she wanted to do: she was infected with the desire for the lost luxury and grandeur of the family, and the symbolic acts she envisioned brought her into this fantasy world.

(Before she could tell Paul she was returning to the house, he ⎞ saw a rabbit and killed it. Miranda admired her brother's skill in skinning rabbits, and she often had Uncle Jimbilly tan the skins so that she could make fur coats for her dolls. She did not enjoy playing with dolls, but she had been taught that luxurious tastes were rightfully hers. Miranda was then too innocent to see the connection between the destruction of the fur-bearing rabbit and the fur coat, between slavery and the ante-bellum family plantations, just as she could not see that the "dark scarlet, sleek, firm" flesh of the rabbit was now prematurely destined to decay.

The children found in the dead body of the rabbit (Paul refers to the rabbit as *it* instead of *her,* thus unsexing the animal) unborn rabbits, each tiny thing enveloped in a "scarlet veil." After the membrane had been removed, they could see them clearly, the down "like a baby's head just washed." Upon seeing them, Miranda instinctively knew the process of birth; Paul buried the babies in the mother, wrapped her in her skin, and hid the body in the sage brush. He swore Miranda to secrecy about the events of the hunt, for he did not want his father to think he was introducing her to things she should not know.

Miranda, true to her new-found knowledge, did not tell and finally put the incident into the grave of her mind. Almost twenty years later, obviously in Mexico, while she was going through a market, the smells of decay and a tray of sugar sweets in the shape of tiny animals, including baby rabbits, plunged her into a Proustian re-creation of the long-forgotten scene. She could smell in the market—which by extension becomes the world, just as the circus tent does—the long-ago scent of sweetness and corruption which brought to her mind the incidents and the knowledge she had gained that day. In the midst of teeming life and rapid decay and confronted by the Indian vendor with his visible symbols of fertility, Miranda sees clearly the implications of these almost forgotten incidents.

Through this concluding frame of the story, all of the themes are brought together; and it is clear that Miss Porter is showing that Miranda has learned that life is doomed to death but that one's reaction to this knowledge is important. At first, Miranda was horrified when she remembered the grave and the rabbit; her reactions to death were quite different from those of the grandmother, who was possessive, who moved her husband's body, and who planned a conventional, late-Victorian burial ground. The father did not discuss such things as the connections between birth and death, and Miranda's new knowledge had to be kept secret from him. Sober Paul (his name suggests the Apostle Paul) had seemingly known about birth all along but had not told her. Her vision in the market was to see that long ago she had learned that life is subject to corruption and death, that life builds on other life and on death, and that the world is filled with chaos, disaster, and destruction.

As her horrible vision faded, she saw her twelve-year-old brother still standing in the blazing sun, smiling soberly, turning the flawed dove in his hands. This second image in the market is a return to the symbol of the flawed innocence of her brother Paul.

The corruption-filled market in a strange city of a strange country dramatically highlights the wandering career of Miranda, who could not accept family legend and tradition; could not accept the usual settled life, as we learn in "Old Mortality"; and found herself an alien in a corrupt world.

"Old Mortality"

The title "Old Mortality"[10] (1940) is from Sir Walter Scott's *Old Mortality* (1816), which begins with a description of John Paterson, known as Old Mortality, a religious enthusiast who wandered the Scottish countryside, caring for the graves of Covenanters killed by the last two Stuarts. He sought out obscure graves, cleaned moss from the stones, renewed the inscriptions, and repaired the emblems of death. He thought he was fulfilling a sacred duty, and superstition had it that gravestones he renewed would not decay again. The Rhea family had a set of Scott's works, we are told in "The Source," and it is obvious that Scott's work was an influence upon Miss Porter—just as Scott's romances had an important part in shaping attitudes of Southerners, as Mark Twain and others have noted. On a symbolic level, Miranda cleansed the past just as Mortality renewed the stones; in her account of her reaction to the past and its myths, she immortalized her own view, the family view, and Eva's view.

The short novel begins on a note of ironic contrast of beauty and impermanence. Both Miranda and Maria heard adults say, on seeing the photograph of now dead Amy, "How lovely." True, her picture was spirited-looking, but she was caught in the "pose of being photographed, a motionless image in her dark walnut frame. . . ." The background of the picture seemed faded and Amy's costume appeared old fashioned, just as the finery much loved by Grandmother Rhea did.

In Part I: 1885-1902 of the story, the children heard the family legends about Amy (literally, "the beloved"); and, while the children were observant enough to see that some details of family legend were untrue, they went on believing. Miranda even believed that Mary, Queen of Scots, died on stage the night of the performance. Obviously, then, she could believe that romantically consumptive Amy would toy with Gabriel's affections, would cause men to fight over her, would copy her Mardi Gras ball dress from the Dresden china shepherdess in the parlor. The grandfather, returned from the grave for this story, ordered her to make her costume more respectable. Amy objected that he had been looking at the Dresden shepherdess for years, but art and life were different to Mr. Rhea.

Amy obeyed but appeared at the party dressed even more daringly. Harry, Mariana, Harry's fiancé and perhaps a romantic rendering of Mary Alice, Harrison's wife, and Gabriel all watched Amy's behavior with some dismay; for young men, some of rather dubious character, flocked about her. Later that night, a former suitor named Raymond, dressed as Jean Lafitte, arrived, went onto the gallery with Amy, and according to family legend may have kissed her, thereby causing Harry to defend her honor by shooting Raymond and causing Gabriel to challenge the pirate to a duel. The events have the overtones of a Sir Walter Scott-influenced romantic, Southern novel. The legend went on and on: Harry's flight to Mexico, Amy's dramatic ride with him to the border, Gabriel's being sent away, Gabriel's being disinherited, the wedding of Gabriel and Amy, their honeymoon in New Orleans, Amy's death six weeks after the wedding.

These stock scenes, presented to the children as reality, are challenged in Parts II and III. Part II, set in 1904 after the death of the grandmother and after the children have been sent to a convent school, begins with a contrast of the anti-Catholic stories about nuns immured in convents and killing their babies, and the sedate, dull convent life the girls lived and saw about them. The girls had to give up trying to fit the violent stories to life. They were immured in the convent, but in a sense not meant in the trashy anti-Catholic novels they read in the summer; they were "hedged and confined," isolated in their muslin-curtained cells at night (just as Stephen was confined in *A Portrait of the Artist as a Young Man*), cut off from the outside world except on Saturday afternoons when they were allowed, if they had not broken too many regulations, to attend the races. "Immured" gave a feeling of glamor to their dull, sterile lives.

The Saturday they met Gabriel, Miranda began to have doubts about the mythic figure she had long heard of; instead of the romantic figure of family legend, he was a fat, red-faced man (as was Joyce's Gabriel, from whom Miss Porter seems to have taken the name) whom Miranda recognized immediately as a drunkard. He was still infatuated with the myth of Amy, a myth which had ruined him. After his horse Miss Lucy won the race, at a hundred to one odds, the children saw the trembling wild-eyed horse, saw the horse's nosebleed, which was a reality far removed from Miranda's romantic view of racing. The scene is a counterpoint to Miranda's shedding her romantic picture of Gabriel.

Taken to see Miss Honey, Gabriel's second wife, Miranda found that, contrary to her name, Miss Honey was sharp, vinegary. At the slum hotel in Elysian Fields (used symbolically, just as Tennessee Williams did in *A Streetcar Named Desire*), they met Miss Honey who all her married life had been compared unfavorably with Amy.

The girls were not then able to connect their dismay at seeing the myth of Gabriel destroyed with the Amy legend; their great disappointment was in learning that their money was to go into the bank, where it was, as far as they were concerned, lost.

In Part III Miranda re-evaluates the legend after her confrontation with Cousin Eva, who like Eve, brings knowledge; and Miranda vows not to be bound by the myths of the older generations. Miranda, now eighteen, was returning to Texas to attend the funeral of Gabriel, who was faithful to Amy to the last and chose to be buried by Amy instead of Miss Honey.

In the sleeping car, Miranda sat with Cousin Eva who told Miranda another story about Amy. Suffering from her ugliness and from being the daughter of a beautiful woman, Eva had never had a romantic view of Amy, never regarded her as a ravishing beauty. She hinted at the scandal surrounding Amy and spoke openly of Gabriel's unhappiness during the honeymoon. Tuberculosis, she said, was not romantic; Amy was driven to her illness by the sexual rivalries of the late Victorian times, Eva insisted. When Miranda repeated the family version of the events, Eva called her a "poor baby" and "innocent" and announced that knowledge would not hurt, that Miranda should not continue in a romantic haze. Eva, an amazingly complex character, perhaps speaks more of the truth than the family had; but, more importantly, she brings knowledge.

The next day, upon arrival, Miranda's father held her at arm's length, for he could not forgive her elopement. Eva and Harry forgot Miranda, for they belonged to the same generation; they had shared memories, and the iconoclasm of Eva seemed to disappear as she and Harry gossiped.

As is true of most of Miss Porter's stories, "Old Mortality" ends in isolation and desolation; it concludes with a definitive statement bringing together the incidents and making clear the symbols of isolation. In Parts I and II, Miranda seldom spoke to anyone; Miranda's sister is in many scenes, but the two sisters seem almost entirely separated; the scenes describing life in the convent and with Miss Honey and Gabriel in Elysian Fields emphasized the feeling of isolation; and Eva, breaking the fiction of the past, made Miranda even more apart from family and past. Miranda then could ask herself where was her time and her place, but she had no ready answer. Secretly, she thought she would free herself from the family and the past, would not even remember them.

She rejected the stories Harry and Eva were telling, rejected the relatives gathered for the funeral of Gabriel, whose life, Harry said without irony, "was just one perpetual picnic." Miranda knew that she could not go back to her husband and his family; family ties, she thought, inundated her with love and with hatred. She was, at this point, Prospero's daughter intent upon making her own discoveries. She wanted, before setting out into the brave new world, to bid farewell to the past by sleeping in her old room.

The revelations of Eva were not completely unexpected; Miranda had previously had doubts. But, when she found she could no longer believe in the legend of the past, she thought she hated. love, although she realized she had to find out herself if she did.

The stories of the past are being told in the back seat of the automobile as Miranda, seated in the front by the Negro driver, tries to fathom the meaning of the past and her own way of looking at it. The final thoughts are, however, heavily weighted with irony: "I don't want any promises, I won't have false hopes, I won't be romantic about myself. I can't live in their world any longer, she told herself, listening to the voices back of her. Let them tell their stories to each other. Let them go on explaining how things happened. I don't care. At least I can know the truth about what happens to me, she assured herself silently, making a promise to herself, in her hopefulness, her ignorance."

The myth of the South, a hint at another reality, self-knowledge, and self-deception are among the most important themes of the story. If *the* truth about events and people is not revealed, at least some of it is; and the gravestones of the past are cleansed, renewed, and preserved.

III *Miranda the Woman*

"Pale Horse, Pale Rider"

And I looked, and behold a pale horse: and his name that sat on him was Death, and Hell followed with him. And power was given unto them over the fourth part of the earth, to kill with sword, and with hunger, and with death, and with the beasts of the earth (Rev. 6: 8).

When "Pale Horse, Pale Rider"[11] was being adapted for a television play, Miss Porter told an interviewer:

"I was quite young during World War in Denver and I had a job on *Rocky Mountain News*. Bill the city editor (the city editor of her story is named Bill), put me to covering the theaters.

"I met a boy, an army lieutenant, . . . Our time was so short and we were much in love. But we were shy. It was a step forward and two steps back with us . . . I was taken ill with the flu. They gave me up. The paper had my obit set in type. I've seen the correspondence between my father and sister on plans for my funeral . . . I knew I was dying. I felt a strange state of—what is it the Greeks called it?—euphoria . . . But I didn't die. I mustered the will to live. My hair turned white and then it fell out. The first time I tried to rise to a sitting position I fell and broke an arm. I had phlebitis in one leg and they said I'd never walk again. But I was determined to walk and live again, and in six months I was walking and my hair was grown back."

"And the boy, Miss Porter?"

"It's in the story." At the sudden memory she fought back tears—and won gallantly. "He died. The last I remember seeing him . . . It's a true story . . . It seems to me true that I died then, I died once, and I have never feared death since . . ."[12]

Although this interview is overdramatic, Miss Porter earlier told Robert Van Gelder much the same story: that she had influenza during the epidemic and was near death. She believes, Van Gelder reported in an interview, "that it is true that the moment of death holds something like revelation." The novel was Miss Porter's attempt "to record that experience," and it was "the best story she has yet written."

The opening scene, a dream sequence, states important themes in the novel: rejection yet love of the past and knowledge and rejection of death. In her early morning dream, Miranda rejected Fiddler, her grandmother's horse, and Miss Lucy, Amy's horse, for Graylie. Gray, the color of her chosen horse, indicates her own ambivalent feelings, although her reason for choosing Graylie demonstrated her wish to win the race with death and the devil. "I'll take Graylie because he is not afraid of bridges," she had thought in her dream, and it is obvious that she had in mind the folk belief that the evil spirits dared not, as Burns's Tam O'Shanter knew, cross a running stream. The green stranger was well known in the Rhea household, and had "been welcomed by" grandfather and by a distantly removed aunt, a young kitten and an old hound. In not mentioning the grandmother, does Miranda, even in her dream, preserve Sophia Jane from death or does she imply Sophia Jane did not welcome the stranger? There had been too much "storied dust" in the household, too much ancestor worship, too many conventions and deceptions, and yet the past was all she had. The stranger rode beside her easily, but Miranda shouted that she would not go with him "this time," fully aware that there would be another time.

Awake, Miranda's non-dream world was just as nightmarish as her dream world. The war was on, with its pestilence and death; influenza was sweeping the country; professional patriots were attempting to force Miranda to spend money she did not have for Liberty Bonds; at the theater she was forced to hear an emotional, dishonest speech by another bond salesman. Added to all this was the limbo of her work, which stretched from afternoon until late at night—a round of reviewing plays and vaudeville acts, of having to face the seedy has-been whom she panned, of work on a newspaper printing the rumors and propaganda of the war, of working with a tubercular sports writer constantly having to explain why he was not at war, and of having a city editor who was a parody of city editors. Over all of this was the war itself. The key to many of these scenes is found in Miranda's thoughts at the theater: "we dare not say a word to each other of our desperation, we are speechless animals letting ourselves be destroyed, and why? Does anybody here believe the things we say to each other?"

Miranda found stability and peace with Adam Barclay, the young Texas-born officer who came by accident to the same rooming house where Miranda lived. The descriptions of him, on a realistic level, emphasize his handsomeness and his masculinity; but, on a mythic level, he is also Adam the first man, made from a bar of clay; Isaac, subject to sacrificial slaughter; Apollo, a handsome young man. Adam, masculinity personified, was still embarrassed at wearing a wrist watch, was completely removed from the world of poetry; and it was Miranda who was able to intuit and prophesy his death. When she saw his face in a bad light, she had a glimpse of an older Adam, "the face of the man he would not live to be."

Miranda could not voice her premonitions, could not tell Adam, as they danced in the tawdry hall, of her pain or of the searing question, "why can we not save each other?" Nor could she tell him of the dumb show—of the young couple in the corner, who, after tears and kisses, settled whatever problem they had and sat looking at each other "into the hell they shared." Contrasted with the dumb show and Miranda's interpretation of it was the conversation she could hear at the next table: a young girl telling her date how a young man gauchely tried to seduce her by getting her drunk. The grossness of the seducer and the narrator contrasted with the incident which Miranda observed but did not hear is a brilliant scene of appearance-reality, which is ever-present in the novel.

From the first dream at the beginning of the story, Miranda was infected with the plague that was sweeping the country. With the illness ravaging her mind and body, the feverish atmosphere became more intense; and she had fewer and fewer lucid moments. Adam came to look after her; but she would talk, then drift off, transported into the perpetual snow of the mountains, chilled to the bone by cold; and, seeking warmth, in her dream she entered into tropical scenes combining her early memories of the grandmother's farm—including the hovering buzzard, described in "Noon Wine: The Sources"—before sailing from this unreal but known world to a jungle. She set sail on a river, a combination of all the rivers she had known and, symbolically, the river Styx; and the jungle was a place of death, filled with animals, bathed in a sulphur-colored light, with rotting trees in the slime. Waving to herself in bed—saying good-bye to her physical body—she sailed into the jungle, with voices crying out danger and war.

Not wanted by the Sisters in the Catholic hospital, or by Mrs. Hobbe, owner of the rooming house, Miranda, thus doubly rejected, tried to talk to Adam about her life, often drifting into the past tense. Neither could talk specifically about the past. Miranda did not speak of her grandmother or her first husband, she did not know whether she had been happy, she had lived and hoped, but was always preparing for a future. Only when she talked of the joys of colors and sounds did she feel strongly about living and use the present tense.

Afraid to go to sleep, Miranda wanted to sing the old Negro spiritual she had heard sung in the cotton fields. She and Adam sang, "Pale horse, pale rider, done taken my lover away," a thematic restatement from the first dream. All were taken away by death except the singer, left to mourn, Miranda knew. Both Adam and Miranda were singing, and they could not know which would be spared.

After the two confessed their love for each other, Miranda again drifted into a dream, a dream in which arrows kept striking Adam, who fell, then arose, to be struck again. The Freudian phallic interpretation is obvious, as is the echo from the myth of Osiris. Miranda, attempting to shield Adam from perpetual death and resurrection, was struck through the heart—with Cupid's arrow—but Adam fell dead.

Finally taken to a hospital, Miranda in her highly feverish state would not believe that Adam had come to see her; and, in a dream, she saw Dr. Hildesheim, who was attempting to save her life, as a poisoner and murderer. Ironically, Miranda subconsciously believed the anti-German propaganda which she could reject when conscious. She tried to explain to the doctor that she did not mean it, but she was swept into unconsciousness again. Wandering in her dream toward oblivion, she found herself without feeling, without attributes. Literally and symbolically, she was at the point of death.

In *Images of Truth,* Glenway Wescott has written that the vision of heaven which follows was one which Miss Porter had much trouble with. "She told me," Wescott wrote, "that she herself, at the end of World War I, had experienced this part of what she had created this heroine to experience and to make manifest; and because, no doubt, it really was heaven, she found herself unable to re-see it with her lively, healthy eyes." Wescott urged her not to try, since heaven is indescribable; but Miss Porter did make the attempt and did succeed. In her mystical vision, Miranda found quiet instead of the noise of the jungle, serenity instead of violence, purity instead of corruption, understanding instead of separation. She found the soft green meadow (much the same as the one in Blake's "The Chimney Sweeper" in *Songs of Innocence*). Miranda was, however, repulsed by the colorless sunlight; she would not accept life under the rainbow, God's gift to Noah.

She became conscious again on Armistice Day and heard old crones singing patriotic songs. She did not know how she would be able to bear the drabness of the world after the reality of her mystical dream, for in the world she now felt the grayness and was acutely aware of her alienation. She did not mean to live in the world and yet could not will her death. Nothing she would ever see would rival "a child's dream of the heavenly meadow."

Society conspired to bring her to health again; her acquaintances came, and she was able to make idle conversation with them, to go through the formal rhetoric of a sick visit. The friends brought her mail, which she put aside for a few days. Forced by the nurse to read the letters, Miranda learned of Adam's death and knew that she was the agent of it and that she had returned from death because she wanted to be with him; but he was at that moment already dead.

Miranda made her symbolic preparations for entering the world of withered beings who believed they were alive: cosmetics for her mask, gray gauntlets for protection, gray hose without embroidery—the gray is consistent with her feeling about the world she is about to enter and is thematically connected with the gray horse of the first dream; it is also a rejection of the mourning clothes which her grandmother habitually wore—and a walking stick. Sarah Youngblood concludes her study of the story: "Her mental image of herself as Lazarus come forth with 'top hat and stick' is a dual vision of herself as he has been and as she will be in the world where appearances must be maintained. . . ." Left to mourn the lover taken away by the pale rider, Miranda at first tried to call into her presence the ghost of Adam (a scene reminiscent of Gabriel's vision of Michael Furey at the end of "The Dead") but failed. Her conscious fears were put aside as she accepted a world without war, houses without noise, streets without people, and "the dead cold light of tomorrow." She knew, as one initiated into both heaven and hell, life and death, "Now there would be time for everything."

Born into a world seemingly stable but in decay, disorder and disruption, Miranda lived at first under the protection of the grandmother who by force of will tried but never succeeded in bringing order to the world of the home and to the larger world of the family farm. Curious to know but generally uncomprehending the full nature of her discoveries, Miranda learned of the glories of the South and the tradition of chivalry, but she also heard of the misery of the Negro; she saw the grandmother's constant companion move away from the demanding Rheas after the death of Sophia Jane; she learned something of the social order of rural Texas and of the mysteries of the womb and tomb; she was afraid of the weeping sound which was connected in her mind with death but accepted a scientific explanation; she romantically dreamed of being beautiful, of reliving the aristocratic past of the family but found that she had to reject the myth of the past as told by her family and as seen by the more realistic Eva; she herself lived in a romantic dream and eloped from a confining convent but had to leave her husband in order to find her own truths; at the age of twenty-four she lived in an utterly chaotic world at war but found in the midst of death that death could no longer frighten her; upon being the agent of death for her lover, to whom she had ironically returned from near death, she covered her sadness with a despair beyond weeping. When we see an older Miranda, a Miranda who had gone gladly into a brave new world, she stood in a tropical market of a strange city, surrounded by bustling life and physical decay, confronted by an Indian vendor selling sickly sweet candied baby animals, and she saw at that moment a vision of her initiation into some of the mysteries of the world. Heaven and hell, love and sex, love and hate, truth and mendacity, life and death, order and disorder—all these are distinct parts of the experience of Miranda.

CHAPTER *4*

To Tell a Straight Story

THE STORIES which follow are divided into four sections. The stories in the first group have a Southern or Southwestern setting, and many have recognizable autobiographic details. "He" and "Noon Wine" have the familiar Southern setting but are concerned with poor whites instead of the aristocratic Rheas. "The Jilting of Granny Weatherall" seems to have been begun as a fictional version of the death of Katherine Anne Porter, but the portrayal is quite different from the fictionalized rendering of Mrs. Porter in the Miranda stories. "Magic" is set in New Orleans, a city Miss Porter knows well, and is a brilliant Jamesian experiment in point of view. The next three stories are "Rope," a universalized rendering of the battle of the sexes; "The Downward Path to Wisdom," one of her most dazzlingly written stories; and "Theft," perhaps a perfect story. These stories are not obviously autobiographical, but their personal tone calls for their inclusion after the first group.

The third group of stories includes "The Cracked Looking-Glass" and "A Day's Work," stories about Irish immigrants in the United States. These stories are, as Professor Marjorie Ryan pointed out in "*Dubliners* and the Stories of Katherine Anne Porter," "Joycean in techniques as well as in theme." Miss Ryan notes that the stories are an "objective rendering of the situation," that the author does not comment, and that, in general, "the meaning is implicit in the action."

The last group of stories concerns Germany and Germans. In the recently published story "Holiday," the reader sees German immigrants in Texas, as they are viewed by a deeply troubled young woman with characteristics much like those of Miranda.

The last story is "The Leaning Tower," written while *Ship of Fools* was still in embryonic form, but the subject matter is Germany of 1931, just after the fictional *Vera* landed in Bremerhaven. Instead of Jenny Brown, the artist, in Berlin, we see Berlin and the Berliners through the consciousness of Charles Upton, who is a sensitive observer.

I *Southern, Southwestern, Autobiographic*

"He"

"He"[1] (1927) was Miss Porter's first attempt to deal with a hopelessly deformed or mentally incompetent person and his place in society or in the family, a theme later explored in "Holiday" and with Herr Glocken in *Ship of Fools*. "He" is told with objectivity, stressing the irony of the situation but ending with compassion for both mother and child.

The Whipples (the name suggests a whip) were a poor Southern family not willing to admit they were "white trash," a family rather like the Thompsons in "Noon Wine." Mr. Whipple was a realist, ready to talk to neighbors about their hard life, but his wife insisted on pretending otherwise—just as she pretended love for their simple-minded son. She announced her love for Him to everyone she saw, and the neighbors were so busy with their own analyses of the bad blood which had produced such a child that they did not have time to notice that her professed love was a cover for hatred. She constantly allowed Him to climb trees, to do more work than He should, to handle the bees because He didn't seem to notice the stings, to lead a dangerous bull, to steal a pig from its ferocious mother. She was never concerned for His safety, except to wonder what the neighbors would say if He were injured.

Mrs. Whipple and He are the chief characters of the story; Adna and Emly (as with Hinry in the Miranda stories, these spellings approximate the pronunciation), Mr. Whipple, and the neighbors are minor but necessary figures who make significant contributions to the action and the theme of the story. He never seemed to mind not having enough cover on His bed or enough warm clothes to wear on cold days, because He had no mind. He was covered with fat, more a harmless beast than a human; and, when Mrs. Whipple killed the pig for Sunday dinner, the description of the pink pig is almost the same as descriptions of Him.

Mrs. Whipple desired public approval; she wanted everybody to tell her that He was not bad off; she wanted her two normal children to be fed and dressed properly, and she wanted the approval of her brother and his family when they came to dinner.

Even had it been offered, He was beyond human help; He could work as if He were a beast of burden, taking on the chores of Emly and Adna who left the "hard times" on the farm. One winter near Christmas (the unwary are warned not to fall into the trap of identifying Him with Jesus) He fell on the ice, thrashed about in a fit, and was carried into the house. When He had had a serious illness, obviously pneumonia, some years before, the Whipples had waited two days before going for the doctor; but this time His suffering was more obvious, and though they had gone for the doctor immediately, He was beyond help. The Whipples kept Him at home for a time, but the doctor finally told them to take Him to the County Home. Was this advice given on humanitarian or mercenary grounds? The Whipples did not know; it was true that Mr. Whipple was relieved, for oppressed by his poverty, his constant concern was with the bills. He was, however, realistic enough to believe the doctor who said He would never get better.

Mrs. Whipple, who didn't want charity, was at first afraid the neighbors would look down upon them, but her true feelings were expressed when she saw her dream of life: "All at once she saw it full summer again, with the garden going fine, and new white roller shades up all over the house, and Adna and Emly home, so full of life, all of them happy together. Oh, it could happen, things would ease up on them." He would not be there.

When a neighbor drove Him and Mrs. Whipple to the County Home, He began to cry, and Mrs. Whipple imagined He was remembering all the mistreatment and hardships of His life. Mrs. Whipple cried too, and for the first time the reader has compassion for her: "she had loved Him as much as she possibly could, there were Adna and Emly who had to be thought of too, there was nothing she could do to make up to Him for His life. Oh, what a mortal pity He was ever born."

Cruel, foolish, vain, and hypocritical as she had been, she had instinctively fought for her normal children, covering her hatred for Him thinly with Christian piety. But her last thoughts stripped the false morality away. It would have been better had He not been born. Even the neighbor driving the carryall, driving very fast to get them to the County Home, dared not look back at the suffering Mrs. Whipple trying to soothe her son. He, beyond help, could receive but could not return love. The Whipples were too human and too poor to be able to do more than they did for Him. The Müllers in "Holiday" never are shown identifying with Ottilie for they had forgotten their kinship with her. They were, however, less outwardly cruel to her than the Whipples were to their son.

"He" is a particularly bleak story, for the corrosive effects of poverty and of a mentally defective child, combined with the bleakness of the seasons—many of the scenes are set in the fall or winter—and the constant reference to Him, spoken as if He were a deity instead of a hopeless creature, are combined into a completely pessimistic story.

"Noon Wine"

The setting for "Noon Wine"[2] (1937) is a small South Texas farm from 1896 to 1905, roughly the same time that Miss Porter lived in that region. The story opens, with a stranger's appearance at the farm of Royal Earle Thompson, a proud man engaged in the disagreeable task of churning. The stranger, seeking work, was hired, and for the next few years Olaf Helton helped make the farm prosper; he was a reticent man who played the same tune over and over on his harmonica.

Nine years after Helton arrived, another stranger came, a Homer T. Hatch looking for Mr. Helton. While Mr. Thompson was talking to Mr. Hatch, they could hear Helton playing the harmonica, playing the tune which Hatch identified as a "Scandahoovian song." "It says," he reported, "something about starting out in the morning feeling so good you can't hardly stand it, so you drink up all your likker before noon. All the likker, y'understand, that you was saving for the noon lay-off." Hatch had come to return Helton to the asylum, to which he had been committed after killing his brother in a fight over a harmonica.

Perhaps thinking that Hatch was going to injure Helton, Mr. Thompson killed Hatch and, like the Ancient Mariner, kept trying to explain to his neighbors just what happened. One night after an all-day trip to explain the killing, Mr. Thompson had a nightmare, and Mrs. Thompson cried out, "Oh, oh, don't! Don't! Don't!" Mr. Thompson, like Claudius, cried "Light the lamp...." The two sons rushed into the room, believing that Mr. Thompson (once a murderer always a murderer) had attempted to harm their mother. "You touch her again, and I'll blow your heart out," one son said. Mr. Thompson, at this moment, felt utter defeat; he had known that his neighbors did not believe his story; now, he saw, his own sons did not believe him. He said he was going for the doctor, but instead he took his gun, went into the field, and wrote: "Before Almighty God, the great judge of all before who I am about to appear, I do hereby solemnly swear that I did not take the life of Mr. Homer T. Hatch on purpose. It was done in defense of Mr. Helton.... I have told all this to the judge and the jury and they let me off but nobody believes it. This is the only way I can prove I am not a cold blooded murderer like everybody seems to think." And then he killed himself.

In "'Noon Wine': The Sources" Miss Porter has attempted to show how an artist lives a story three times: "first in the series of actual events that, directly or indirectly, have combined to set up that commotion in his mind and senses that causes him to write the story; second, in memory; and third in the re-creation of this chaotic stuff."

She remembers when she was a child hearing one late summer afternoon, when the sky was "clear green-blue with long streaks of burning rose in it" and filled with swooping bats, the sound of a thundering shotgun, and a long-drawn out scream. "How did I know it was death?" she asks, and replies, "We are born knowing death. Later she remembers watching the hearse go by and members of her family saying: "Poor Pink Hodges—old man A.... got him just like he said he would."

When she was about nine, she noticed a strange horse and buggy in the drive and saw a man and woman inside the house, talking to her grandmother, the woman "in a faded cotton print dress and a wretched little straw hat," a woman with the marks of "life-starvation" all over her. She kept her eyes on her twisting hands as her husband in a coarse voice said, "I swear, it was in self-defense!... If you don't believe me, ask my wife here. She saw it. My wife won't lie!" And the wife answered each time, "Yes, that's right. I saw it." Though Miss Porter never knew the facts of the killing or the outcome, she knew that the woman was made to lie; that she did it unwillingly; but that her husband, dishonest as he was, made her lie in an attempt to make his lie true. This man was not, like the man in the story, "foolishly proud" but "a great loose-faced, blabbing man full of guilt and fear."

Not long afterwards, Miss Porter was with her father when they saw a "tall, black-whiskered man on horseback, sitting so straight his chin was level with his Adam's apple," with a flamboyant black hat on the side of his head. Her father said, "That's Ralph Thomas, the proudest man in seven counties." She asked what he was proud of, and her father replied, "I suppose the horse. It's a very fine horse." And she saw then that the man was ridiculous and yet pathetic.

On another trip she saw "a bony, awkward, tired looking man, tilted in a kitchen chair against the wall of his comfortless shack,... a thatch of bleached-looking hair between his eyebrows, blowing away at a doleful tune on his harmonica... the very living image of loneliness. I was struck with pity for this stranger, his eyes closed against the alien scene, consoling himself with such poor music." Later, she learned he was a Swedish farm worker.

Miss Porter explains the process of memory and artistic creativity which she used in the story:

> I saw ... a few mere flashes of a glimpse here and there, one time or another; but I do know why I remembered them, and why in my memory they slowly took on their separate lives in a story. It is because there radiated from each one of those glimpses of strangers some element, some quality that arrested my attention at a vital moment of my own growth, and caused me, a child, to stop short and look outward, away from myself; to look at another human being with that attention and wonder and speculation which ordinarily, and very naturally, I think, a child lavishes only on himself.

[88]

In "Noon Wine" Pink Hodges is merged with the Swedish farm worker who becomes the "eternal Victim"; the whining man, the Killer, is merged with the proudest man in seven counties; the Killer's wife, a pathetic figure, becomes the genteel Mrs. Thompson.

Mr. Thompson (even the name is significant here—he is one of Tom's sons—one of the plain people, but with the pretentious name Royal Earle) has married slightly above himself. Mrs. Thompson, in her gentility and ill-health, is typical of her time; she is ironically named Ellen—that is, Helen, Goddess of Beauty. She is bound by a moral code, dictated by a frontier religion which she finds immutable. Mr. Thompson sees himself as a murderer and makes his wife lie, hoping the lie will alter the fact; but she too, as the boys do, thinks him to be a murderer. By making her consent to lie, he has murdered her spirit; but she can never do more than publicly lie—she can never help him redeem himself by telling the final lie, by insisting that she really did see, that he did kill in self-defense.

Mr. Thompson's motives were mixed; Helton had brought a better life to the Thompsons; Mr. Thompson did not want his new prosperity damaged. Hatch was obviously an evil man, and all of society agreed that Mr. Thompson should not be punished. The courts would not convict him, but he was still a murderer.

The name Hatch, again, is particularly appropriate, since he has come to return Helton to the booby-hatch; even his given name Homer (who was blind) is significant, for Hatch is a man blindly working within the law, with no regard for the suffering of Helton. Helton, suggesting Hell tone or the sound of Hell, is a man beyond good and evil; a murderer; his own victim and the victim of others.

Miss Porter does not allow Miranda to tell the story because Miranda could be no more than an observer, and the differences in social positions removed her too far from the tragic events of the Thompson family. "Noon Wine" belongs to the time and place of the Miranda stories, but for artistic reasons it is not one of them.

The setting of the story is near Buda. In Texas, that name is pronounced almost as if it were Buddha, and the first half of the story is filled with Buddhistic peace and quiet; however, the town was not named for the Oriental deity but is a corruption of the Spanish word for widow. Mrs. Thompson is near widowhood from the moment Hatch arrives at the farm.

"Noon Wine" is concerned with one of the central problems in Miss Porter's fiction: the efforts of man to cope with evil. None of the Thompsons is fully capable of understanding or opposing the evil of Hatch and the evil he left behind or the good-evil of Helton. Mr. Thompson never understands his motives in killing Hatch and is driven to his own self-murder. Mrs. Thompson cannot tell the ultimate lie which would save her husband. The Thompson boys believe the worst of their father. Helton has largely overcome his psychic malaise, or rather his compulsion to do violence; but he lives in a private hell which no one can understand. Hatch's motivations cannot be explained away in terms of the financial rewards he received; he is the evil principle, beyond understanding. "There is nothing," Miss Porter says, "in any of these beings tough enough to work the miracle of redemption in them."

"The Jilting of Granny Weatherall"

"The Jilting of Granny Weatherall"[3] (1929) may be seen as another of Miss Porter's creations utilizing her "usable" past—as a somewhat more objective, even more fictional presentation of the actual grandmother. Or, one may extend the story as a part of Miss Porter's use of "historic memory," as Ray B. West has called it, and therefore see that the death "reflects a particular, but common, attitude toward death." More recently, John Hagopian has found the moral "to be that the universe has no order, the proper bridegroom never comes—to expect him will inevitably lead to cruel disillusionment."

The story is presented by an omniscient observer who reports the stream of consciousness of the dying Ellen Weatherall. During the last day of her life, old Granny Weatherall, almost eighty, moved back and forth from consciousness to unconsciousness, from the present to the past, conjuring up all her old fears and old dreams. Similar to Miss Porter's fictional Grandmother Rhea, Granny Weatherall had been a strong-willed, active woman who had buried a young husband and reared a large family. Mrs. Weatherall had for sixty years, however, been trying to forget that on the day of her proposed marriage, her first fiancé, George, had jilted her. She had married John later, borne his children, and named the first one George; but the last child, the one she wanted to have by George, she called Hapsy—quite obviously a diminutive of Happiness.

The morning of her last day of life, she could still play her role as a cantankerous old woman when the young Dr. Harry (curiously enough the name of Miranda's father) came. She could still focus her eyes, could still hear the whisperings of Dr. Harry and Cornelia, although things did seem to float, and the whisperings sometimes took on strange sounds, as if they were leaves outside. Back and forth in time she went, thinking of her orderly house, the clock with the lion on it which gathered dust (a reference to James's "The Beast in the Jungle")—that is, the disorder which she, like Sophia Jane, constantly had to fight. She plagued dutiful Cornelia with whom she lived (the name reminds one of King Lear's Cordelia) but wanted Hapsy, the daughter now dead. She wanted to see her first fiancé, to tell him about her husband and her children: "Tell him I was given back everything he took away and more. Oh, no, oh, God, no, there was something else besides the house and the man and the children. Oh, surely they were not all? What was it? Something not given back!"

Her thoughts extend her loss to the same loss explored in James's short story, and even her name is similar to Weatherend, the name of the house where the James story begins. Some of the descriptions are similar; May Bartram's household was described by James: "The perfection of household care, of high polish and finish, always reigned in her rooms, but they now looked most as if everything had been wound up, tucked in, put away...." Miss Porter wrote: "Things were finished somehow when the time came; thank God there was always a little margin over for peace: then a person could spread out the plan of life and tuck in the edges orderly. It was good to have everything clean and folded away...."

Granny tried to delude herself into believing that there was nothing wrong with her, just as she had deluded herself about being able to forget her jilting. When Hapsy appeared to her, Granny seemed to be herself and "to be Hapsy also and the baby on Hapsy's arm was Hapsy and himself and herself, all at once. . . ." Himself was undoubtedly George, whom she couldn't call by name. Hapsy said, "I thought you'd never come," and they started to kiss; she was then near death, but Cornelia spoke and Granny was called back.

By night, she was barely able to speak or focus her eyes; she was unaware of the meaning of Father Connally's actions as he administered the last rites of the Church: she had a rosary in her hand "and Father Connally murmured Latin in a very solemn voice and tickled her feet. My God, will you stop this nonsense?" Only when she dropped the rosary and took instead the thumb of her son Jimmy did she realize her living children had come for her death. In a panic, she began to think of all the unfinished things she wanted done, and then Hapsy came again. She asked God for a sign, but again there was none. Again there was a priest in the house but no bridegroom—that is, in this second jilting, the absent bridegroom was the Jesus of Matthew 25: 1-13. She could not forgive being jilted again. Willful to the last, she would not be jilted again; she herself blew out the light.

The death scene has many similarities with Miranda's near death in "Pale Horse, Pale Rider," for both emphasize the darkness, the pale light, the grayness. Gray was the color of the fog and smoke which crept over the bright field where everything was planted orderly, and it was the color of George, for the thought of him was "the smoky cloud of hell"; one is reminded of the "grey impalpable world" at the conclusion of "The Dead." As in "Pale Horse, Pale Rider," the grays of death and the green of life are constantly juxtaposed, just as the images of light, the lamp, candles, matches, flame, are contrasted with those of dark, of fear, and betrayal and death. Smoke and fog hid approaching death, but orchards, fields, rows of crops and fruit trees, green rugs and polished floors represented happiness and the joy of life. Granny Weatherall's mind drifted with all of these images, just as Molly Bloom's did in the last section of *Ulysses*; but Molly's answer was "Yes." Granny's affirmation was her own will to die.

As is usual with Miss Porter, the truth is bitter and pessimistic. Her ending, an echo of James again, is fully as horrible as that of John Marcher, who saw the lurking beast, which rose, leaped, missed; to avoid it, Marcher "flung himself, face down, on the tomb." Miss Porter has learned her lessons from James perfectly. Her story has all the finesse, skill, and symbolism of the master himself; but, although she echoes James, the story is uniquely her own.

"Magic"

"Magic"[4] (1928), told by a Negro maid, once a servant in a bordello but now employed in the home of Madame Blanchard, is one of the best examples of Miss Porter's use of Jamesian narrative techniques. The maid was a woman who prided herself on her French blood and her good character, but she worked where work was to be found. Her narrative about a bit of magic at the house of prostitution where she once worked was told to amuse Madame Blanchard, whose hair she was brushing. Madame Blanchard had remarked to the laundress that the sheets wore out so quickly they were obviously bewitched, and the maid had her own story of magic to tell. Acutely aware of her role as an entertainer, the maid in her narrative emphasized the scenes of violence, the peculiar monetary system the Madam used, the exact details of the making of the charm to bring Ninette back. The maid had, she insisted, seen too many things, terrible events which she willingly and frivolously told to her new mistress, a Madame who had only an *e* to distinguish her from the Madam.

Madame Blanchard, a lady with a French name which in earlier times meant linen, the qualities of whiteness and coolness being particularly appropriate, sat at her dressing table, apparently a little bored. The maid hoped, she said, the violent, perverse story she was going to tell would rest her mistress. Madame Blanchard obviously did not object to hearing the story; in fact, at two different times she asked the maid to go on with the story. The first interruption is of special interest: Madame Blanchard complained that her hair was being pulled at the time when the maid was telling that the Madam had a complete understanding with the police and that the girls stayed with the Madam unless they were sick (an obvious euphemism for venereal disease). Later, as more violent episodes were told, one would imagine that the brushing might have become more violent, but Madame Blanchard did not protest. While it may be true that the maid did pull the hair, it is just as likely that the mistress was distressed by the implications of the story, for the institutions of middle- and upper-class life were being undermined, and she may have used the hair pulling as a rather nervous protest. Madame Blanchard, showing no compassion for the prostitutes, was as cold and expressionless as her sheets, qualities which she held in common with the Madam.

As the maid continued with her long narrative about life in the brothel, she and Madame Blanchard provide the frame for the story of a life which was, perhaps, not much different from any other life. The household was controlled by the Madam who had no human feelings, was constantly cheating the girls, arguing over money, fighting by unfair means. When Ninette, the most called-for girl, announced, independently, that she was leaving, the Madam beat her furiously and kicked her in the groin before turning her out into the street. Ninette was engaged in a profession which was, as the narrator saw it, just a business. An outcast of society, Ninette was courageous in defying the Madam, who had the police and pimps on her side; but her revolt was, from the first, doomed.

A magic brew to bring Ninette back was made by the Negro cook, a woman with much French blood, also, but a woman with bad character, the narrator insisted. After the maid had finished with the lurid details of the making of the magic brew, Madame Blanchard interrupted again, thus returning the reader to the frame; closed her perfume bottle, although all the scents of Araby would not wash away the horrible story; and asked, "Yes, and then?" Yes, the maid said, the charm worked; Ninette returned, was ordered upstairs to dress for work.

The narrator's account of the story, toned down in language but with certain of the violent scenes emphasized, is not to be considered the truth, but a dramatic version of what happened. The narrator, for instance, was never aware of the ironies involved: she referred to the bordello as a fancy house; she believed that the magic potion had brought Ninette back; she missed the significance of the man's greeting, "Welcome home," to Ninette on her return. The story ends on a final note of irony: Ninette, who had dared to revolt, to flee the corruption of the sordid house, found no haven in a world itself corrupt and sordid; she returned therefore to the Madam, where she would again be cheated, but where she was in demand by the customers. The maid ended the story as if it were a fairy story and everyone lived happily ever after: "And after that she lived there quietly."

This story of five pages is of great complexity, uniting Jamesian point-of-view; the frame with its characterizations of the maid and the mistress; the story with the Madam, the maid, and Ninette; subtle psychological probings; and bitter social criticism. A major achievement, this story is too little appreciated.

II *Universalized*

"Rope"

The he and she of "Rope"[5] (1928), never identified by name, are tied together in marriage; but, in their love-hate relationship, they are hanging each other, giving one another enough rope for hanging, forcing the other on the ropes, and each is at the end of his rope. The story is another of Miss Porter's examinations of marriage, of love, hate, and frustration. Unlike her other stories dealing with marriage—such as "That Tree" or "The Cracked Looking-Glass"—the exact time, place, and setting and the background of the characters are not known. By implication we know it is late fall, that the setting is in the country, and that both he and she earn money, his income being larger.

The first and last paragraphs emphasize the tranquility of the rural scene. They had only been in the country three days, and already he had told her she looked like a country woman, and she told him he resembled a rural character in a drama. But the hayseedish characters were completely deceptive, and the tranquility soon disappeared, not to return until he came from the store the second time. Ostensibly, she began the quarrel because he forgot to buy coffee, and she had not had coffee that day. He had instead bought a rope, and the rope soon became the center of the argument; he had bought it impulsively, could think of no real use for it.

The indirect quotations emphasize the bitterness of the quarrel which was unraveling their marriage. The rope had broken the eggs; she had no ice to keep them until the next day; she would not have the rope in her pantry. He didn't know what tied them together, why he shouldn't just clear out. She reminded him of the casual affair he had the summer before. Like Miranda's grandmother, she was too busy organizing the house to enjoy the country; he, paraphrasing Emerson, didn't think the house should ride them. He returned to the store, two miles away for her coffee, for her laxative, and for the other items she suddenly remembered. He took the rope to exchange it, but secretly hid it behind a rock.

When he appeared again, rope in hand, masculine pride still intact, she had completely changed; she was waiting serenely for him, supper ready, not concerned at all that he had "forgotten" to exchange the rope. She was playful, kittenish, talking baby talk. The last paragraph derives much of its poignancy from the veiled reference to Whitman's "Out of the Cradle Endlessly Rocking" in which the he-bird sat calling for the never-to-return she-bird. Miss Porter's use of he and she may have been influenced by Whitman's poem, although she also uses the names to give a universal, an Everyman-Everywoman effect. They heard a whippoorwill, still there out of season, sitting in a crab-apple tree—fittingly sour fruit—"calling all by himself. Maybe his girl stood him up. Maybe she did. She hoped to hear him once more, she loved whippoorwills . . . He knew how she was, didn't he?" She projected her own feelings into the sad song of the bird, imagining that his mate had jilted him, wanting to hear the bird's song again.

The story ends with a note of tranquility masking the terrible battle which had just been fought. They had both said too much that could not be forgotten, and many of the threads of the rope holding them together had been unraveled. The final line indicates that the husband was also aware of the implications of the quarrel and of her interpretation of the bird's song: "Sure, he knew how she was." The disastrous quarrel in "Rope" is similar to the corrosive Jenny-David affair in *Ship of Fools*.

"The Downward Path to Wisdom"

"The Downward Path to Wisdom"[6] (first published in *The Leaning Tower*) begins with another of Miss Porter's ironic contradictions: instead of an ascent to wisdom, Stephen travels downward in his journey from innocence to experience, from blissful ignorance to knowledge, from paradise to hell. An examination of the fiery furnace of childhood, the story concentrates on a few weeks in the life of Stephen, who is called by his correct name late in the story, for he most often was called "baby" or "fellow" or "bad boy."

Stephen, at the opening of the story, was a four-year-old child described and treated as if he were an animal: when he was lifted into his parents' bed, he sank between them "like a bear cub in a warm litter"; he crunched his peanuts "like a horse." His peanut-eating reminds one of the monkeys in "The Circus" and of Otto in "The Leaning Tower" who was beaten as a child because his mother did not like the sound of cracking walnuts. The story contains many echoes of Joyce's *A Portrait of the Artist as a Young Man*: Stephen as Stephen Dedalus, Stephen's meow and Stephen Dedalus' being told the story about a moocow; Stephen's being jeered at by the schoolchildren when he tried to make a meow; Stephen Dedalus' being pushed into the square ditch; Stephen's father with a tough (hairy?) chest and Stephen Dedalus' father with a beard; Stephen's eating peanuts and Stephen Dedalus' being given a cachou.

The rejection of Stephen takes several forms: his mother doesn't like peanut shells spilled all over her, and he was put out of bed and finally out of the room while his parents quarreled over his eating the nuts—an argument as pointless and at the same time as pointed as the one in "Rope." Since the whole story is reported from Stephen's point of view, the reader does not know exactly what went on between the parents, only how it affected Stephen.

Rejected by both parents, he was soon rejected by the maid Marjory, who called him a "dirty little old boy" because he didn't want his breakfast; she even repeated what we learn later was the family opinion of Stephen's father—he was mean. The fight between the parents became so intense that Stephen was sent suddenly to his grandmother's house to stay. He was frightened, even though he had been sent to her house before; the only comforting thing he could think of was his peanuts, and he cried for them.

Stephen's hostility toward the world was a natural reaction: he could never be certain of the reactions of those around him. His father had given the boy the peanuts and then scolded him for eating them. His Uncle David gave him the balloons but turned on him when he took others without permission; the old grandmother, seeing all the hate building up over the boy, finally declared that she just wanted to be left alone; the old servant Janet who took him to school made him feel guilty about sex.

All of the adults had been expelled from paradise themselves, and the crucial scene in the story is Stephen's expulsion. At school, Stephen met Frances, the archetypal Eve. To win her affection, he gave her balloons; but his offerings did not appease her. She was larger and more mature than he; when they danced at school, she wanted him to follow her; she punished him by saying he couldn't dance and then that she didn't like the way he danced. It was she who had the other children look at Stephen's animal which he thought was a cat but which she declared to be a horse. Stephen learned in his first days at school that popularity could be bought with favors but could vanish suddenly, leaving him a scapegoat, a figure to be ridiculed.

The balloons he and Frances sat blowing on one Saturday swelled, changed colors, became part of his dreams and aspirations; but they grew and grew, only to burst, a final disillusionment. Stephen chose an "apple-colored" balloon and Frances took a "pale green one," perhaps representing the green fig leaves used by Adam and Eve after they tasted the apple. They were still in paradise: "Between them on the bench lay a tumbled heap of delights still to come." Frances—her name can be, with a slight change of spelling, masculine or feminine—bragged of a beautiful long silver balloon she had once had (the images become phallic in this scene); but Stephen urged her to go on playing with the round ones they had. He felt of his ribs and was surprised not that he had lost a rib for the creation of Eve but that the ribs stopped in front. Frances was growing tired and restless, just as Eve did. Stephen pushed the "limp objects" toward her and urged her to go on enjoying the delights they had, the millions more that would last and last. Instead, she wanted other delights: "a stick" of licorice to make "liquish" water. Stephen didn't have any money, but Frances was persistent; she was thirsty, and she might have to return home. To keep her, Stephen promised to make lemonade. He took the forbidden fruit and made the drink, putting it into a teapot; to keep the adults (God) from knowing, Stephen suggested they go to the back garden, behind the rose bushes. Frances ran beside him like a deer, "her face wise with knowledge," as Stephen ran with the teapot. They drank from the spout of the teapot—a phallic image again, and in keeping with her rejection of limp balloons and request for a stick of licorice—playing games, letting the lemonade run over them. Finally full, they began to give the rosebush a drink, and Stephen baptized it in the "Name father son holygoat," making the Christian ceremony pagan again.

Caught by the maids, Frances looked at her shoes and let Stephen take the blame. Stephen, in this scene, left babyhood, left innocence, and his route paralleled the Old Testament account of man, expelled from the garden and free to follow strange gods.

Uncle David made a great scene about the theft of the balloons, called the boy a thief, railed against Stephen's father. The grandmother made no real attempt to protect the boy; she agreed with David that Stephen should be sent home, but hypocritically referred to Stephen as "your Grandma's darling."

When Stephen's mother arrived, she quarreled with her mother and brother; but it was a histrionic scene ending with a promise to come for a visit in a few days. Stephen, stripped of all of his innocence, didn't want to go home to his father, who had rejected him; but his mother carried him to the car. In the front seat, rejected and frightened, without love or comfort, initiated into the ways of the world, Stephen sang to himself: "I hate Papa, I hate Mama, I hate Grandma, I hate Uncle David, I hate Old Janet, I hate Marjory, I hate Papa, I hate Mama. . . ." He had started over and had not yet mentioned Frances. The story does not end with this terrible song, but with Stephen growing sleepy, resting his head on his mother's knee. She drew him closer; he could be her love; she drove with one hand, obviously caressing Stephen with the other.

The martyr Stephen, in the sixth and seventh chapters of Acts, reminded the multitudes that they would not accept the message brought by Jesus and that they always persecuted the prophets. True to his prediction, he was stoned to death. Miss Porter's Stephen was martyred; he was driven into exile just as Joyce's Stephen was. Stephen Dedalus went into exile in France at the end of *A Portrait* and had just returned from that country at the beginning of *Ulysses*. Could not *Frances* be a play on *France?* And could it not be that the balloons are a subtle reference to the wings of the original Daedalus?

"Theft"

"Theft"[7] (1929), one of Miss Porter's most subtle and complicated stories, is told from the point of view of a no-longer young writer, supporting herself largely by writing reviews. The central character of the story has much in common with the unnamed, alienated narrator in "Hacienda." The setting is the New York bohemian world, perhaps in the 1920's; the characters are insecure and poor; and the mood is sad, gloomy, dismal. In the opening scene, the lateness of the hour, the desolate Elevated station, the driving rain, set the tone for the story.

She declared the clearness of her memory and the value she placed on the purse: she had put it on the wooden bench the night before and had dried it. The next day when she realized the purse was gone, she began to think about the events of the night before. Camilo, a graceful young Spanish acquaintance, had walked her to the Elevated station in the rain, even though his new, biscuit-colored hat was being ruined. She saw Camilo as one who used most effectively the small courtesies but ignored "the larger and more troublesome ones." Somewhat intoxicated, her thoughts were on the impractical hat, which would now look shabby; and she compared Camilo's hat with Eddie's— always old, but worn with "careless and incidental rightness." She had no intimate relationship with Camilo, no real concern about him except for his hat. She saw him at the corner putting his hat under his overcoat, and she felt that "she had betrayed him by seeing," though this is certainly her interpretation of the event and may be only partially true.

Before she could get to the Elevated, Roger called to her; and the scene with him is perhaps the most pleasant one of the story. They were old friends and perhaps lovers; he readily admitted the bulge under his coat was his hat being protected— the hats help reveal the characters of three of the men—and she willingly shared a taxi with him. His arm around her shoulders was comforting, and it was obvious their relationship had been an amiable one. Stopped at a light, she saw, and in her recollection she comments on, two scenes: three young men, in "seedy snappy-cut suits and gay neckties" arguing about marriage, the first maintaining he would marry for love; the second wanted him to tell that to the girl; and the third insisted on the sexual connotations: "Wot the hell's he got?" The first had defended his manhood: "I got plenty," and they had squealed and scrambled away. She saw them not as human but as scarecrows, and her use of "gay" as a description of their neckties may have been her subconscious attempt to de-masculinize them. She also saw, at the same stop, two girls, in transparent raincoats; and the girls were, in a way, transparent to her. One girl said, "Yes, I know all about *that*. But what about me? You're always so sorry for *him*..." She saw them not as humans, but as rushing by on "pelican legs."

Later, Roger told her that Stella was returning, that all was "settled." She said she had had a letter too, but things had been settled for her. Roger, self-reliant, when asked about his show, announced he wouldn't argue about things; they would have to take it on his terms or abandon it. He borrowed a dime to help pay for the fare, and told her to take aspirin and a hot bath to ward off a cold.

Upstairs, she visited Bill, a self-centered, weak writer, without the outer strength of Camilo or the inner strength of Roger. He complained about paying alimony, was oblivious to the fate of his child, refused to pay her the $50 promised for her help on his play. She let him steal her money, without a real objection. Upstairs she had read the letter, obviously from Eddie, accusing her of destroying his love for her. She tore the letter into strips, and her actions demonstrated clearly that her alienation from those around her sprang from herself. In destroying the letter, she destroyed her last link with Eddie.

She then remembered that the next morning the janitress had come in while she was having a bath, saying the radiators had to be looked after before turning on the heat; and the janitress had sometime later gone out, "closing the door very sharply." When she returned to the room, the purse was gone. She dressed and made coffee, her excitement and anger growing. She put the cup down in the center of the table (emphasizing the religious ritual) and descended into the basement to demand her purse from the janitress, who was at the furnace and streaked with coal dust. The scene that followed was that of an inferno. The woman first denied stealing the gold-cloth purse. The writer attempted to reassert herself, to act positively, instead of giving in, as she had done with Bill. As she confronted the janitress, she remembered that she had never worried about possessions, that she had been indifferent and careless with them, that she had not loved them just as she had not loved or been able to go on loving others; she had therefore given others the chance to rob her. Then the physical act became a symbol to her: "she felt that she had been robbed of an enormous number of valuable things, whether material or intangible: things lost or broken by her own fault, things she had forgotten and left in houses when she moved: books borrowed from her and not returned, journeys she had planned and had not made, . . . the long patient suffering of dying friendships and the dark inexplicable death of love"; all of these she had lost and was losing again in memory. Her anger and her desire to get the purse back had been a desire to keep from losing herself. The woman returned the purse, first saying, with "red fire flickering in her eyes," that she had a seventeen-year-old niece who needed a pretty purse, and then that she must have been crazy to have taken it.

The janitress argued that her niece was young and needed her chance; the writer had already had hers. The writer tried to return the purse to the janitress, who said spitefully that the niece didn't need it because she was young and pretty: "I guess you need it worse than she does." The writer was then caught in a circular trap, never able to keep from causing her own alienation, her own losses. The janitress had the last word: the purse was being stolen from the niece.

The writer put the purse on the table again, but the coffee (sacrament) was chilled. The purse was on the altar, but the woman knew that "I was right not to be afraid of any thief but myself, who will end by leaving me nothing." All of the incidents of the story are chosen to emphasize this final view. The alienation is pointed up by the rain and its effects on Camilo, Roger, and the writer; she saw that the rain changed the shape of everything. Stairs would have taken her to the Elevated (and the life of the spirit); she went down the stairs into the basement, a trip into a heart of darkness, where she saw the fire-filled eyes of the janitress and had the first intimations of the real nature of the theft.

The primary symbol in the story, which unites all the story, is the purse and the woman's feelings about it. At first, it was a material possession, a birthday present probably from Eddie; and therefore it represented their past relationship and its dissolution. The purse, at the beginning of the story, was almost empty, for she was both physically and spiritually poor. The janitress forced her to take the purse, but she had decided she no longer wanted it; she had physical possession of that which she had lost, but was haunted by all the symbolic losses. This final irony is perhaps the most bitter of them all; for, after her descent into hell, she has seen her own tragedy and the tragedy of all men—but in the meantime the wine of the sacrament (coffee) had become chilled.

The search for both profane and sacred love are the important themes of this complex story. The narrator rejects Camilo; loses Roger to his wife; is cheated by Bill, a blasphemer; and causes Eddie to reject her. She did not take the Elevated, or spiritual way, but descended into a hell, and found upon returning from the depths that the modern sacrament was unsatisfactory. She was left with a gold purse and cold coffee, a wasteland figure without any kind of love.

III *The Irish*

"The Cracked Looking-Glass"

Stephen Dedalus said of the mirror Buck Mulligan stole from a servant: "It is a symbol of Irish art. The cracked lookingglass of a servant." Brother Joseph Wiesenfarth has recently pointed out that the mirror symbol in Miss Porter's story was a reference not only to Joyce, since Rosaleen had formerly been a chambermaid and practiced the Irish art of self-deception, but also to Tennyson's Lady of Shallot who wove her web while observing through a mirror the life outside the tower. Likewise, Rosaleen observed herself through a mirror and often worked on a tablecloth which apparently would never be completed. Miss Porter may also have had in mind I Corinthians 13:12, "For now we see through a glass, darkly; but then face to face." Brother Wiesenfarth in his perceptive study sees that the mirror symbol, central to the story, changes constantly, encompassing "the imagination of Rosaleen, the imperfection of human love, the necessity of accepting that love as it is, the marriage of Rosaleen and Dennis, reality, the difficulty of knowing reality. . . ."

"The Cracked Looking-Glass"[8] (1932) is filled with Joycean techniques and allusions. Rosaleen, an Irish woman, was similar to Molly Bloom in being married to a man no longer sexually satisfying to her; like Molly, her son had died; and without son, without husband-lover, she had taken literally or in spirit other lovers. It is not quite certain how many young boys she had had in the house: Kevin had been with them for a year but had gone away when Rosaleen became jealous of his young girl friend after seeing the girl's picture. Rosaleen asked Hugh Sullivan to come live with them, but he declared that it was too dangerous. And a neighbor extended the whole field of promiscuity: "A pretty specimen you are, Missis O'Toole, with your old husband and the young boys in your house and the traveling salesmen and the drunkards lolling on your doorstep all hours——" Although the reader sees events and characters from the point of view of both Rosaleen and Dennis, he never finds any final statement, never reaches an absolute truth.

The story is an account of Rosaleen's progression from illusion to reality. Thirty years younger than Dennis—the name is ironic because it is derived from Dionysus—Rosaleen was sexually starved and constantly improved on stories, Irish fashion, to make the grim reality of her existence more endurable: the story opens with an account of her Billy-cat and his death which she learned of in a dream. Dennis showed the story to be a fabrication; like Mr. Bloom, Dennis was an outsider because he had grown up not in Ireland but in Bristol, England; and he considered himself "a sober, practical, thinking man, a lover of truth." As observer, though, Dennis has his weaknesses; he was filled with self-pity and could not see that Rosaleen had changed in the twenty-five years they had been married. He lived almost entirely in the present instead of the past.

Rosaleen lived much in the past, because it could be improved upon in memory and in story. She thought of her girlhood in Ireland as a great triumph, and she still longed for men to fight over her. Instead of the glorious green past, she had in reality a farm in Connecticut, an old husband growing senile, and her own fading looks. In her dreams, she triumphed by having others die; she dreamed that Kevin, the housepainter, did not write because he was dead; she dreamed the Irish boy she could have married was dead. When she had to face actual death, she put aside the grim reality by dreaming about it, as she did after the great-grandfather's death.

The most important episode of the story, the one that shocked Rosaleen back to reality, was her trip to Boston to see her sister Honora, whom she dreamed was dying. Life on the farm was grim, and the dream gave her a chance to escape, a pretext for an adventure away from the small village. Instead of going directly to Boston, she went by way of New York, where she had lived with Dennis, who had been a headwaiter at a hotel. She saw, as part of her adventure, two romantic films: "The Prince of Love" and "The Lover King."

In Boston, she discovered her sister had moved, without leaving an address, dramatic proof that her dream was not true. She also found that Hugh Sullivan, a young Irishman, either understood exactly or completely misunderstood her invitation to come to the farm. Her dream of having a young man in the house was shattered, and she was left with the reality of living out her life with Dennis. Guy Richards (his name suggests Grant Richards, the publisher, with whom Joyce had many unpleasant dealings), the local drunk, was her last hope of escape from her life with Dennis. She wanted him to visit her, but he did not; and again her dream was shattered.

She had forgotten to buy a new looking-glass, and with the acceptance of the old glass, she accepted her life and marriage. Life was "a mere dream," she thought, accepting that too; and she put aside the dreams of the green field of her youth. She asked Dennis why he had married her, and he replied that he could not have done better. Suddenly, she felt solicitous, wanted him to keep warmer, and said she didn't know what would happen to her when he was gone. Dennis turned from the reality of his death, saying, "Let's not think of it," and she agreed not to do so, ending compassionately, "I could cry if you crooked a finger at me." Rosaleen had accepted the reality of their life; but, in order to go on living, they could not think of the future, of his approaching death. The story ends on the same note of despair on the human condition that one finds in many of Miss Porter's other stories. The poetic Irish language, the realistic details, and the literary echoes are superbly combined in this complex, subtle story.

"A Day's Work"

"A Day's Work"[9] (1940) is more than a story of the battle of the sexes or another of Miss Porter's investigations of marriage, as some critics have seen it. It has as its setting the slums of New York during the depression, and as a social background the political corruption of Tammany Hall. Mr. Halloran, a past middle-aged Irish immigrant from whose point of view we see much of the story, had been fired from his job in a grocery store two years before his retirement, ostensibly because of the depression but more likely to avoid paying him his pension. For seven years he had been sitting at home, drawing his relief money and listening to the complaints of Mrs. Halloran, who added to their income by doing washing and ironing. He was as cantankerous as she, always talking back, constantly provoking his shrewish wife. He was particularly bitter because he had wanted to go into politics—and the numbers racket, closely allied—but his wife wouldn't allow it. Mrs. Halloran had, as McCorkery the political boss had predicted, held Halloran down, but, in holding him down, she had kept him out of the rackets.

Mrs. Halloran, puritanically religious, had disapproved of McCorkery and his fast crowd but had approved of Connolly, a good Catholic with nine children. Halloran learned from a policeman that Connolly was wanted by the G-Men because of his criminal activities; Halloran, completely amoral, objected to police meddling, and the policeman, corrupted by the system, wanted to know what the harm was: "A man must get his money from somewhere when he's in politics. They oughta give him a chance." On the way to the saloon, Halloran imagined what might have been if his wife had let him work with McCorkery, and he dreamed of what it would be like when he talked with McCorkery, telling him of his dismal home life and his willingness to help get out the votes, now that election time was near.

The dream and the reality came together violently, for McCorkery was at the bar, and Halloran did ask for a job. While McCorkery was in a back room with some of the boys, Halloran was even more depressed by what might have been after seeing the prosperous political boss; he drank too much and dropped the whiskey bottle—reminiscent in many ways of the opening scene of Joyce's "Grace." McCorkery, needing votes, was outwardly calm when dealing with his old crony who was a failure; his voice was loud and hearty but had a curse in it; he slipped money to Halloran and sent him home by taxi.

At home, Halloran was repulsed by his wife. She appeared in his alcohol-induced state as a ghost in a "faded gingham winding sheet," and her voice was "thick with grave damp." He threw the iron at the "devil" advancing toward him and then fled into the street and told a policeman he had killed Mrs. Halloran. Before they could investigate, Mrs. Halloran appeared and told the policeman she had fainted and struck her head on the ironing board. She helped her husband upstairs, threw him on the bed, wet a large towel, tied knots in the end, and began to strike him in the face, at each whack calling out his offense: drunkenness, stealing, walking in his stocking feet, his part in raising their daughter. (The scene is remarkably similar to the *Ship of Fools* scene in which Mrs. Treadwell strikes Denny in the face with her shoe.) As symbol of her victorious assault, she wound the wet towel about her head, knot over shoulder; put the money from McCorkery in her locked metal box; and called her daughter to announce, for the neighbors to hear, that Halloran had a job. All her objections to the political boss had disappeared.

Illusion and reality come together forcibly and ironically in this sordid, black comedy, filled with mellifluous Irish phrases. Miss Porter managed to capture the sterile, hate-filled lives of the Hallorans, and she brilliantly etched in the political machinations of two Tammany leaders, the corruption of the ward itself, and the corrosive effects of the depression. She presents, as Marjorie Ryan has shown, the "strange, violent life in a society as dead on the surface as Joyce's." In addition to a moral landscape similar to Joyce's *Dubliners* stories, Miss Porter also introduces characters named Gogarty and Finnegan, instantly recognizable to those who know Joyce's life and work.

The psychological probings and the rhetorical dialogue are especially noteworthy, and this realistic story of the depression in the New York slums deserves to be better known.

IV *Germans*

"Holiday"

The aristocratic Hans in "The Leaning Tower" announced that, when he spoke of Germans, he did not mean peasants; Tadeusz the Pole replied, "Perhaps we should always mean peasants when we speak of a race . . . the peasant stays in his own region and marries his own kind, generation after generation, and creates the race. . . ." Miss Porter presents such a race in the Müller family, third generation Americans, but still German peasants.

"Holiday"[10] (1960) is told by an unnamed narrator who, long after the events had happened, recalled them. The sensibilities and the background of the narrator are similar to Miranda's. The thesis is stated in the first paragraph: the narrator was too young for the troubles she was having, and her family background and training had not taught her that it was possible to run away from some things. She had learned later the difference between courage and foolhardiness; but, when the events of the story had taken place, she did not then know "that we do not run from the troubles and dangers that are truly ours, and it is better to learn what they are earlier than later. And if we don't run from the others, we are fools."

The narrator, wishing to escape her problems, which with the passage of time had diminished and need not be described, had gone, on the recommendation of Louise, a school friend, to the East Texas farm of the Müller's. Louise had described the family and the farm romantically, but the reality the narrator confronted was quite different. Left on "the sodden platform of a country station," she was taken in a dilapidated wagon through bleak country to a forbidding farmhouse, set in an infertile spot. The fat puppy of Louise's story had turned into an enormous, detestable beast.

When she arrived at the front door, the whole family, except the father, came out, and the narrator saw that they all had the same eyes, the same "taffy-colored hair," even though two were sons-in-law. She found herself in a patriarchal society, in which Papa Müller and the men were treated with deference and respect, the wives standing behind their husbands at meal times to fill their plates.

The story seemingly moves slowly, as the narrator observed the customs of this farming family with deep roots in the soil. Deeply conservative, almost completely isolated from the mainstream of American life—in fact from most community life except for Saturday excursions to the *Turnverein*—the family formed its own little closed society. The narrator found that Papa Müller was a student of Marx, and yet he was the richest member of the community. She observed the disciplined children at play, a wedding, a birth, a funeral—the life cycle of the family.

All of the realistic details (the story is filled with animals and animal imagery) suddenly took on more meaning when the narrator discovered that Ottilie, the crippled, dumb servant girl, was actually one of the Müller children. She worked constantly, as if she were in perfect health, preparing the vast quantities of food consumed by the Müller family: she worked because the work had to be done, and because she could do it. John Hagopian in *Insight I* has speculated that in naming Ottilie, "Miss Porter had in mind the Ottilie Home for Crippled Children in New York (an obvious juxtaposition of *Ottilie* and *Crippled*) named after the saint in Alsace, who was born blind but whose sight was restored on baptism." Ottilie showed the narrator a picture of herself as a healthy little girl, tried to speak, but could not. The past in the picture was frozen, but the picture brought the two together. For a moment, the narrator thought, Ottilie knew she was Ottilie, "knew she suffered," staggered away, significantly leaving the picture face downward. Later that day, Ottilie regarded her as a stranger, but the narrator could not let Ottilie be a stranger.

In immediate juxtaposition is a long account of the family's treatment of animals: the boys trapped wild animals, the girls tended the animals and chickens tenderly; Frau Müller's death resulted from her overexertions in tending to the animals during the storm. The Müllers had put Ottilie out of mind, the narrator thinks, though this may not be all the truth in this matter; and, out of self-defense, they forgot her.

The compassion for Ottilie is shown with great restraint, however, and is contrasted with the emotional scenes of the Müllers after the death of Mrs. Müller. Even Ottilie was caught in the emotionalism, for the narrator who had stayed alone in her room the day of the funeral, filled with the "terror of dying," heard strange noises, and found Ottilie howling in the kitchen. The narrator hitched horse to wagon and started after the funeral procession. But they were too far behind, and there was no hope that Ottilie could be made a member of the family for that day, or even that Ottilie wanted to join the family circle.

Something, perhaps the sky or the turning wheels—the narrator never knew—suddenly filled Ottilie with joy. It was definitely spring, the flood had caused a profusion of vegetation (certainly the Müllers could understand only in a literal sense that April is the cruelest month), and the scene, in which they sit, horse stopped, surveying the woods and the heavens, is a variation on Frost's "Stopping by Woods on a Snowy Evening." The narrator pondered her mistake: "There was nothing I could do for Ottilie, selfishly as I wished to ease my heart of her; she was beyond my reach as well as any other human reach, and yet, had I not come nearer to her than I had to anyone else in my attempt to deny and bridge the distance between us, or rather, her distance from me?" She knew they were both fools of life, both fugitives from death, and, as a celebration, they took a holiday. Ottilie (not the horse, as in Frost's poem) had become fidgety during their pause, but they started again, taking, significantly, "the small road divided from the main traveled one"—again a Frost allusion. The irony, compounded by the overtones from Eliot and Frost, is especially heavy as the narrator thought they would be home in time for Ottilie to prepare supper and nobody need know of their holiday.

The meaning of the story, John Hagopian has said, "is simply this: that man lives in a universe without shape or meaning. He is therefore obligated to project a meaning, to shape and form his own life in an effort that is ultimately doomed since it will end with death and chaos. But while he is making the effort, he can be sustained by love—even love for a twisted, mute, half-beast of a human being like Ottilie. Since we are all prisoners of the universe together, let us love one another." Richard Poirier, in his introduction to *Prize Stories 1962: The O. Henry Awards* ("Holiday" won first prize), has a reading far different from Professor Hagopian. To Poirier, "The story is about people whose communal labor has created relationships among them and between them and their natural environment, so close that literally nothing except death can disrupt them."

The Müllers had dealt with Ottilie realistically.: they had given her an importance in the household, a central position; but they had forgotten their blood ties, their spiritual ties. Their position was at the same time cruel and practical. Neither Christianity nor Marxism had taught the Müllers compassion. One can, then, read "Holiday" as a political parable, as Miss Porter's probing of the German question: she describes German clannishness, materialism, cruelty, love of animals and mistreatment of fellow human beings, and a willingness to put out of mind the unpleasantness of the past—characteristics she also has described in "The Leaning Tower" and *Ship of Fools*. Whether read as personal narrative or as political parable, the conclusion is a sobering one: the narrator, although she was giving Ottilie a holiday, could do little for the girl; for the narrator's own holiday would end soon. She would then leave the Müller farm, leave Ottilie and the Müllers to their fate.

"The Leaning Tower"

"The Leaning Tower"[11] (1941) may properly be introduced with some journal notes by Miss Porter in December, 1931. A young poet she knew in Berlin objected that she should not bother reading Rilke's *Elegies*: "He belongs to the old romantic soft-headed Germany that has been our ruin. The new Germany is hard, strong, we will have a new race of poets, tough and quick, like your prize fighters." The poet gave Miss Porter some of his poems, and she found that the "words were tough and the rhythms harsh, the ideas all the most grossly brutal; and yet, it was vague weak stuff in the end."

In another note that December she described a conversation with L. and von G. about Nietzsche: "Nietzsche is dangerous because his mind has power without intelligence; he is all will without enlightenment. His phrases are inflated, full of violence, a gross kind of cruel poetry—like Wagner's music. They both throw a hypnotic influence over their hearers. But I could always resist hypnotists. When I think of Nietzsche and Wagner, at once by simple association I find charlatans of all kinds and degrees. . . . And madness. In Nietzsche's case, a real, clinical madness: his diseased brain gave his style the brilliancy of a rotting fish. L. and von G. worship them both with a religious awe." Finally she could not listen, but she captures in 1941 in the short novel much of the spirit of that impression and rumination of 1931.

In January, 1932, still in Berlin, Miss Porter wrote that R. always spoke about religion, but that he was a man filled with maliciousness, one who spoke evil of everyone. He told her that she could know nothing of the higher levels of religious experience because "Religious experience belongs exclusively to the masculine principle." Without seeing the irony of his words, he assured her that "Only ample, generous natures are capable of the love of God." Miss Porter does not use these philosophical and religious and esthetic statements in "The Leaning Tower," but she does incorporate the malignity in German society which she was aware of and writing about in her journal in 1931 and 1932.

The novel may be divided into five major parts: the café as a place of memory, of Charles's childhood illusions of Germany and the reality; the search for a new room and the exit from the hotel; the new room and the inhabitants of the pension; the night club; and the final revelation in the room. Charles Upton, the central character, from whose point of view we see the events, is given a background similar to Miss Porter's. Sensitive but, like Miranda, naïve, he came from a Central Texas farming family with Kentucky ties; and he had, against the initial wishes of his family, been interested in art—just as Miss Porter, against the wishes of her family and society, had determined to be a writer. He had come to Berlin largely because of his boyhood friendship with Kuno Hillentafel, whose mother was alleged to have been a countess. Through a romantic projection of Kuno's descriptions, Charles had imagined Berlin to be a great city of castles towering in the mists.

Alone in the strange city of Berlin that Christmas season, left with his memories of Kuno, who had died on one of the trips to the homeland, Charles had found the city depressing; he escaped his hotel and sat in the café where he could see clearly the illusion and the reality. Among the heavy buildings were heavy, pig-like people or slim young students all dressed alike; he had seen in his few days in the city the desperate poverty of the country, the streetwalkers, and the beggars. His impressions had been harsh and poignant: he had seen fat Germans peering at displays of candied pigs, pig worshipers holding up their dachshunds to see the display, and he had had a poverty-stricken, fearful shopkeeper sell him wrong-sized socks because she had to make a sale. The shock of being in a strange city and culture had unsexed him, and he had been unable to show interest in the streetwalkers. His impressions were not ordered, allowing him to generalize about the German society which he found disturbing. His was not a reflective mind; he was storing his impressions for his drawings, drawings which could be brutally accurate, as when he drew the hotel owners: the woman as a sick fox and the man as half pig, half tiger. He felt completely isolated in the society; for, the larger the crowd he found himself in, the more isolated he became.

The rush of impressions subsided as Charles set out to search for a room, for the rooms fell into an easily distinguished pattern of stuffy, faded elegance or of expensive modernity. At the apartment of Frau Rosa Reichl—whose name is particularly appropriate because she had once been rich, employed many servants, but now lived in reduced but not poverty-stricken circumstances—he was impressed by a bare hallway; but the room itself was standard, with heavy drapes and carpets, massive furniture, whatnots. Charles accidentally broke her plaster souvenir of the Leaning Tower of Pisa, a tottering structure in actuality and, in replica, a fitting symbol of a society soon to topple again. Americans had in 1917-18 helped topple German society, and Frau Reichl was not unaware of the significance of Charles's act. Outwardly she saw the fragile souvenir as a memento of her honeymoon, but it had come to be a symbol of the old days that had long passed. Charles knew that she was thinking that she should not have left it out for crude foreigners to touch.

When Charles announced his intentions of leaving the hotel, all civility fled from the hotel owners. He was outrageously overcharged, threatened with police action if he did not pay the bill as it was submitted, intimidated by passport inspection—experienced travelers had told him he would feel like a criminal while traveling in Germany.

The outward brutality and bestiality disappeared once he

moved into Rosa's room. On the day of his move, he learned, in a quiet scene in a barber shop, that a shouting politician (obviously Hitler) had made one particular hair style popular. This third section of the story presents Rosa's apartment and the inhabitants as a microcosm of German society in 1931; but, since Miss Porter has only three Germans, one American, and one Pole, her cast is much more limited than in *Ship of Fools*. Charles said of Rosa and the guests: "They were all good people, they were in terrible trouble, jammed up together in this little flat with not enough air or space or money, not enough of anything, no place to go, nothing to do but gnaw each other." Charles had the best room and paid the most rent because all Americans were thought to be rich. He was, because of this mythic wealth, protected from Rosa's sharp tongue. Her favorite in the house was Hans von Gehring (the name reminds one of Hermann Goering), the aristocratic-looking young man, a student at Heidelberg, where he had fought a duel and was now receiving treatment for his infected wound. Charles wanted to like the young man, but he was unable to comprehend a society which approved such barbaric acts. Charles rejected the wound and everything that allowed it to be possible, even though he had seen the antique dueling pistols of his great-grandfather. Hans was proud of his scar, often fingered it; and Charles saw in the young man's face his true nature: "amazing arrogance, pleasure, inexpressible vanity and self-satisfaction."

Rosa's scapegoat was Herr Otto Bussen, a Platt Deutsch, whose inferior social station and poverty gave Rosa license to intimidate and demean him at every opportunity. That he was a brilliant student at the university made no difference to Frau Reichl. When Herr Bussen poisoned himself, accidentally or otherwise, she was as concerned about her rugs as about his health.

The other lodger was Tadeusz Mey, a Polish-Austrian pianist and a cosmopolitan at home in London and Paris, who was living in Berlin because there was a good teacher there. Mey was constantly aware of the evils in society and was opposing them, but he was cynical enough to study and live in the corrupt German society. He and Charles were the only ones in the apartment with insight into the society, but Charles was the only one with a ready escape: he could always return to his own country.

In his sleep, Charles's premonitions about the society, as personified by the house and its inhabitants, could not be put aside. The house was burning, pulsing with fire. Charles walked from the building with all the paintings he would ever do in his life. When he turned to look back at the burning house, he thought at first that they had all escaped; but he heard a ghostly groan (is this not similar to the "weep" Miranda heard?) and saw not a person. Symbolically, then, Charles knew that he would and could walk away from the society which was destroying itself and its members. His artistic creations were more important to him than any attempt to save the unsavable, to save those who, we must assume, would misunderstand his act and turn on him ferociously. Charles did not even reflect on his dream when he awoke, stifling in the feather coverlets; he did not know exactly what it meant; and he did not think of it when he considered giving an extra coat to Herr Bussen, an act which Mey said would be a great mistake.

The next section of the story moves from Rosa's to a newly opened, middle-class bar where the young men go to celebrate the New Year. In many ways, the section confirms Tadeusz's view that losing the war damaged the "nation's personality," but it goes beyond that to try to search for personality traits which were established long before the war. At the night club, Charles saw another sampling of German society: Lutte, the thin, blonde model, a perfect German type to Hans; the large barmaid, attractive to Herr Bussen; two movie stars; and a large crowd of noisy, sentimental revelers. During the conversation, race was much discussed; and fat Otto, aspiring intellectual, insisted that "the true great old Germanic type is lean and tall and fair as gods."

The conversation then swirled into a long discussion of races and cultures, and Charles, who, like Miranda, had rejected the mythic views of a "splendid past" which his parents had taught him, could not compete in the conversation since he knew almost no history. Drawn into the gaiety of the night, he danced with Lutte, but found she was interested in him only if he could get her to Hollywood. She soon turned her attention to the more aristocratic Hans.

Tadeusz spoke of his family, which had lived in the same house for eight centuries, of the stifling society of his childhood, of the anti-semitic attitudes implicit in the religious dogma; his memories of the past were mixed, "something between a cemetery and a Lost Paradise." Otto, who grew up in a Lutheran family, spoke of his dismal childhood, of building his life on a romantic view of Luther, apparently willing to follow anyone who had become great.

At midnight, a wooden cuckoo announced the New Year; and, after the toast (nobody had been aware of the irony of the cuckoo), a "disordered circle formed"; and there was much singing and drunken revelry until "the circle broke up, ran together, whirled, loosened, fell apart." The tourists' Germany could not last, and the young men had to get the drunken Otto home. Otto—symbolically, his befuddled moribund state was that of the intellectual—was carried past Rosa, who looked at her young men fondly. Charles in his drunken state, saw (or thought he saw) the Leaning Tower, now repaired, behind the glass door of the cabinet; and, though he could not quite understand why, he knew he wanted to crush the frail, useless thing. The meaning of the tower tried to break into his consciousness but could not; he felt a "dislocation of the spirit" because he was beginning to see that the society was going to fall, that it would involve him, and that there was nothing he would do. He did not feel sorry for himself, but he did know that "no crying jag or any other kind of jag would ever, in this world, do anything at all for him."

The story has many brilliantly conceived scenes, and it is not the failure that many critics have charged it to be. Charles has vague portents of the meaning of what he sees; in his dream, he saw that the society was facing destruction. He had learned that his initial reaction to the Germans was true: "They were the very kind of people that Holbein, Dürer and Urs Graf had drawn . . . their late-medieval faces full of hallucinated malice and a kind of sluggish but intense cruelty that worked its way up from their depths slowly through the layers of helpless gluttonous fat."

"The Germans," Miss Porter said in an interview in the March 31, 1962, *Saturday Review*, "are against anybody and everybody, and they haven't changed a bit." Her view cannot, I think, be dismissed as a crude anti-German one, as some have tried to do. In "The Leaning Tower" she was engaged in a literary probing of the German problem, which contains all the material for a study of the nature and the meaning of evil. Her journal entries from Germany give us an indication of what she saw; and she reported honestly in her fiction what she saw.

Each of these stories is an investigation of what Miss Porter has rightly called the "terrible failure of the life of man in the Western world." Her aim as a writer, she says, has been "to tell a straight story," and she has succeeded admirably. These stories, set in the South, in New England, and in Germany, and dealing with poor whites, Irish-Americans, artists, Berliners, German peasants, and many others are a remarkable literary achievement. They are as subtle and perceptive as the best works of Joyce or James.

CHAPTER 5

Ship of Fools

K NOWN by the earlier working titles of "Promised Land"
and "No Safe Harbor," *Ship of Fools* was for years the
subject of much literary gossip. The novel was often promised
but always postponed, and many critics gave up hope that it
would ever appear. Glenway Wescott in *Images of Truth* has
said that Miss Porter set out to create "a large lifelike portrayal
of a numerous and representative society, with contrasts of the
classes and the masses and the generations and the ethnic groups,
with causes and effects in the private psychology of one and
all, and with their influences on one another—every man to some
extent a part of every other man's fate—and all of this made
manifest in behavior, action, plot!" Wescott has written of the
tribulations which beset Miss Porter during the years she was
writing *Ship of Fools*: unfavorable destiny, "passionate life and
personal weakness and disadvantages in the day and age and in
our present heterodox American culture." To these one should
certainly add Miss Porter's need to support herself by lecturing
in colleges and universities across the country and, perhaps, her
fear of publishing a long work.

Even some of Miss Porter's friends lost faith in the novel,
as she went on working on it over the years, publishing not the
work itself but fragments of it in *Harper's, Atlantic Monthly,
The Texas Quarterly* and many other journals—fragments which
did not and could not show the scope of her novel. At one time,
Glenway Wescott wrote, but did not mail, a letter suggesting to
Miss Porter that she should give up the project, salvage what
sketches she could, and move on to other work.

Miss Porter went on working. The short novel which was to
have been included in *Pale Horse, Pale Rider* went on growing
after she began serious work on it in 1941 in Yaddo. After two

months of work, she is quoted as saying in *Newsweek* for
July 31, 1961, that her divorce interfered; and she did not return
to it again until she was in Boulder, Colorado, in 1942, where
she worked for three months. For the next thirteen years, she
worked at it "a page here and there" until 1955; then she rented
a Connecticut house and put in three years of work until lack
of money drove her to the universities again. But in the spring
of 1961 she "finished the whole damn thing in six weeks."

I *American Criticism*

Miss Porter's prepublication interviews in *Time* and *Newsweek*
in July of 1961 are carefully controlled and make no mention of
the problems and self-doubts hinted at by Wescott. But the stage
was being set for her only popular success. Her short stories
deservedly were widely praised, but the general reading public
had never paid much attention to her works. The Book-of-the-
Month Club, however, chose *Ship of Fools* as its April selection,
and in its brochure sent to members published a brief essay by
Glenway Wescott (later published, in expanded form in *The
Atlantic Monthly* and in *Images of Truth*) and an ecstatic
review by Clifton Fadiman, who declared, "here at last is Miss
Porter's *magnum opus*. Not only was it worth waiting for, but
your judges would be derelict in their duty if they did not
wholeheartedly urge it upon the attention of Club members."

Book-of-the-Month Club selection insured wide sales, and the
literary speculation and advance publicity contributed to the
novel's becoming number one on the best-seller list within
weeks of its publication on April 12, 1962. *Publisher's Weekly*
for May 21 carried a note that the publishers, Atlantic-Little,
Brown, had allocated over $50,000 for advertising the novel,
including full page notices in the daily New York *Times* and in
leading American magazines and newspapers and "360 60-second
commercials" on FM radio stations.

Time informed its millions of readers, on April 6, 1962, that
"*Ship of Fools* is a study in despair. The despair is not relieved
by the usual dilutions. . . . In fact there are no personal obtru-
sions, nothing of the gracious, 70-year-old Southern gentlewoman
who in the 20 years since her last book has seemed to occupy
herself chiefly with being a charming chatterer at literary gather-

ings. Her testament is objective and her verdict is unemotional: the world is a place of foulness and fools."

Newsweek published a similar review on April 2, 1962: "Among the lesser things to say about it is that it is the Book-of-the-Month for April. The main thing to declare is that in her full maturity, in a country where high-level fiction is scarce and likely to be fragile, Katherine Anne Porter has produced a work of rugged power and myriad insights, a book of the highest relevance to the bitterness and disruption of modern civilization."

Major American literary reviews were almost as laudatory. Mark Schorer in the lead article in the New York *Times Book Review* (illustrated with a brilliant George Grosz drawing) noted the many delays in publication but concluded that the novel would endure "for many literary generations." Professor Schorer's comprehensive, sympathetic review emphasized the influence of Brant's *Das Narrenschiff* on the novel, the artistic techniques, the strongly developed characters, and concluded that *Ship of Fools* could best be compared "with the greatest novels of the past hundred years. Call it, for convenience, the 'Middlemarch' of a later day."

Louis Auchincloss in a review in the New York *Herald-Tribune Books* on April 1, 1962, also emphasized the novel's Victorian qualities. The review was illustrated with a flattering photograph of Miss Porter by Bradford Bachrach, emphasizing her beauty and charm. The issue also contained an interview by Maurice Dolbier, beginning with a Mexican toast, which Miss Porter translated, "Health and money, more power to your elbow, many secret love affairs and time to enjoy them." The toast was enough to engage the reader's interest and to set the tone for Miss Porter's chat on ancestors, writing, men. She concluded, "I've had a very hard life, but it's not other people who have made it hard for me. I did that for myself. But I've had a good run for my money—a free field in the things that matter: the will to be an artist and to live as a human being."

Not all of the early reviews were quite this favorable; Granville Hicks, in *Saturday Review,* March 31, 1962, entered an early minority report: "It is hard not to judge the book in relation to the extended period of gestation; the temptation is to proclaim that it is either the fulfilment of a great hope or a sorry disappointment. But if it is certainly not the latter, neither is it quite the former. It shows that Miss Porter is one of the finest writers of prose in America. It also shows that she has mastered the form—or one of the forms—of the novel. On the other hand, it is something less than a masterpiece." His final conclusion was that "the novel, for all its lucidity and all its insights, leaves the reader a little cold. There is in it, so far as I can see, no sense of human possibility. Although we have known her people uncommonly well, we watch unconcerned as, in the curiously muted ending, they drift away from us." Accompanying the review was a photograph of Miss Porter, posed glamorously, and an interview by Rochelle Girson, in which Miss Porter stated the theme of her story: the novel, she said, is "the story of the criminal collusion of good people—people who are harmless—with evil. It happens through inertia, lack of seeing what is going on before their eyes. I watched that happen in Germany and in Spain. I saw it with Mussolini. I wanted to write about people in these predicaments—really old predicaments with slightly new political and religious aspects."

Howard Moss in *The New Yorker* for April 28, 1962, and Stanley Kauffmann in *The New Republic*, April 2, 1962, also had reservations; but the inevitable critical reaction set in with Theodore Solotaroff's "'Ship of Fools' & the Critics" in *Commentary* for October, 1962, a debunking akin to Dwight Macdonald's "By Cozzens Possessed" which appeared in the January, 1958, *Commentary*. Solotaroff categorized the central concerns of the reviewers: the personality cult around Miss Porter, the universality of the novel, characters in the novel, and the general breakdown of society. Then, he thought, he demolished their arguments. He objected strenuously to Miss Porter's presentation of Herr Löwenthal, the Jew: "Miss Porter uses him in a situation whose implications are both historically misleading and morally vicious." In fact, he argued, Miss Porter had presented "the stage Jew of the modern literary tradition whom other Christian writers of sensibility (among them T. S. Eliot) have dragged out of the ghetto to represent the vulgar and menacing dislocations of traditional order. . . ."

German critics were later to take up this charge of unfairness, but it was not the presentation of the Jew that annoyed them. Solotaroff concluded that Miss Porter had failed to present an allegory of the "ship of this world on its voyage to eternity," that it was, rather, a labored account of a tedious voyage, revealing to the reader "little more than misanthropy and clever technique."

II English and German Criticism

English critical reception of the novel was definitely cool. Robert Taubman, writing in *The Statesman* of November 11, 1962, complained that Miss Porter had written a dull novel about folly: "the novel fails because it never gets down to more than marginal analysis." The fault lay in Miss Porter's "resources as a writer," he concluded. "If she gets as far as folly and some minor brutalities, she doesn't get as far as evil."

The Times Literary Supplement review for November 2, 1962, admitted that there were moments of "great power and compassion" in the novel, but the review was highly unfavorable: "One may guess at what went wrong. Composed over twenty years, under the impact of a changing, darkening reality, *Ship of Fools* may have become to Miss Porter a complex argument, a provocation to constant technical virtuosity, rather than an imaginative whole. One cannot help wondering whether she *knows* enough—of German history, of the sources of modern anti-semitism, of European middle-class speech and values—or whether that knowledge has penetrated the exquisite, but very special, range of her feelings." The reviewer summed up many of the English critics' objections:

> But the achievements are those of a great short-story writer. They glitter like passages of subtle, concentrated brushwork in a canvas too large and too thinly composed. And that may point to the essential flaw. The allegory Miss Porter has devised is too naive for the literal and moral enormity of her theme. The energies and representative values articulate in the plot are inadequate to the question posed. Moreover, there is no norm, no dramatic centre. The pack of hysterics, alcoholics, thieves, hypocrites and sex-starved weaklings assembled on the good ship Vera stand for no larger truth. The claim of universality lies only in the outward symbolism.

Sybille Bedford in *The Spectator* for November 16, 1962, praised the novel: "The Great American Novel has appeared; ironically, it has turned out to be a great universal novel." But there were also flaws: "the massed detail," the static quality of the novel, and a wavering attitude toward Mrs. Treadwell; but this review is the most sympathetic one which appeared in major English journals.

Angus Wilson, writing in the influential *Observer* on October 28, 1962, put the novel into the middle-brow, book-club formulas of the 1930's: "It is impossible, I suspect, to use such a thumbed-over, middlebrow formula for writing a novel as the bringing together of passengers on a ship without awaking in the reader overtones of other, less-distinguished, novels that have exhausted the device, especially if, like Miss Porter, you lay your scene in the 1930's when that particular genre of book-club middlebrow novel was at its height."

German critics were even more unkind to the novel; but, in general, their objections were political ones. Long before publication of a translation—scheduled for fall of 1963—reviews began to appear. The first was in *Die Welt* of June 9, 1962. In a preface to the review, the editor quoted Marguerite Higgins as saying there is no anti-German movement in the United States, but "understandable resentments" are still to be found. The editor concluded, "These resentments have found their expression in the voluminous, recently-published novel of a prominent American writer, 72-year-old Katherine Anne Porter, which was unusually successful with the critics and the public in the USA. Was this because of its theme or because of its literary qualities?" The headline over the review announced the answer to the question: " 'The Germans are still cruel, evil and fanatic'/Document of Hatred: K. A. Porter's 'Ship of Fools.' "

Although Herbert von Borch's review was less virulent than the headline—in fact, he did see some of the literary problems involved—he unfortunately introduced a political interpretation which has now become a standard judgment of the work in Germany. Making use of Miss Porter's interview in the *Saturday Review* for March 31, 1962, which emphasized that she had watched the rise of fascism in Europe but did not wish to write a thesis novel, he chose instead to begin his quotation with Miss Porter's current views about Germany and the Germans: "they are just as dangerous as they were, and the moment they get back their power they are going to do it again. This complacency about Germany is simply horrifying. . . . The Germans have taken the Jews as a kind of symbol, but they are against anybody and everybody, and they haven't changed a bit!"

Sabina Lietzmann pursued this interpretation in the *Frankfurter Allgemeine Zeitung* on July 16, 1962. Assuming the existence of vast anti-German prejudice in America, she managed to connect the novel with Shirer's study of the Third Reich and Stanley Kramer's movie *Judgment at Nuremberg*, works which did not receive great critical acclaim in Germany. Largely because she failed to see the Brant framework of the novel, she felt the German passengers were treated extremely harshly. *Der Spiegel* on September 12, 1962, used much the same approach as Mrs. Lietzmann and concluded with an amazing standard of criticism: Miss Porter was planning a European vacation to Ireland, Paris, and Rome, but "Her route did not take her through Germany."

Herr Heinz Paechter in "Miss Porter's New Garments" published in the *Deutsche Zeitung* of October 13-14, 1962, used, as part of his attack, Theodore Solotaroff's article in *Commentary*. Ignoring Solotaroff's objections about the unfair treatment of the Jew, Paechter wrote that Miss Porter used the concept of the Nazi as a too-easy symbol of human depravity; he quoted Solotaroff as demonstrating that "out of her masochistic pessimism towards civilization, Miss Porter gives up every discrimination, and that this attitude makes her unable to characterize even the real Nazis in their depravity...."

Norbert Muhlen in *Der Monat* for December of 1962 found that it was indeed true that all nationalities were represented unflatteringly in the novel, but he concluded that this is "the fashionable stereotyped image of humanity which affirms original sin but denies divine grace—an inevitable trade mark of 'sour kitsch' which no longer takes a rose-tinted but a murky view of the world." Herr Muhlen complained that the German characters were clichés, and he objected to Miss Porter's presenting Germans in 1931 as talking of gas ovens, as treating Jews as pariahs, or as boycotting a German married to a Jew. Americans had to be told, he said, that about half of the Jewish marriages in 1931 were mixed marriages, and that, within the commercial society to which Freytag belonged, hardly anyone was discriminated against because of his Jewish wife.

While parts of German reviews have been favorable, the

troublesome political problem almost always was present. As a result, it is obvious that German reviewers were unwilling to admit that any Germans were aboard the *Vera* in 1931.

III *Some Source Material and the Method*

Miss Porter: "I promised myself solemnly: in this book [*Ship of Fools*] I will not load the dice. We all do it. . . . But this time, I resolved, everyone was to have his say. I would not take sides. I was on everyone's side."

Mr. Wescott: "Yes, my dear, but it might also be said that you are on no one's side" (*Images of Truth*, p. 53).

Asked about the unfavorable criticism of *Ship of Fools*, Miss Porter said, "I wrote the book I meant to write." She went on to say that she had always been gently treated by the critics but that, after her first best seller, the critics "came at me with a double-barrelled shotgun loaded with rock salt and carpet tacks, ready to let fly." They missed the point of the novel, she felt, and she said (with resignation or contempt; one cannot quite tell from the context), "I cannot do a thing for them" (New York *Herald-Tribune Books*, October 11, 1962).

Some of the critical confusion stemmed from Miss Porter's own comments on the novel, however. German critics, faced with contradictory statements—the theme of the novel is the collusion of good, harmless people with evil, and Germans are just as evil and dangerous as they ever were—chose the latter and therefore interpreted the novel as propaganda. Mark Schorer agreed with Miss Porter's often quoted comments that she had sympathy for her fools; Solotaroff found her contemptuous of mankind and pointed not to Miss Porter's interviews but to the novel to argue his case.

Although Miss Porter's statements sometimes vary slightly, the general order of the history of the composition is this: The novel began as a long letter to Caroline Gordon, describing the passage from Mexico to Bremerhaven in 1931. Miss Porter kept a journal during the trip, and she continued during the 1930's to work on her notes. She abandoned the original structure, after she realized it would not be a short novel; but she kept the individual episodes, moving them about, and writing new scenes around them. The opening scene, she explained, remained the same, but she later added the dead boy; she had also written in the first version the last scene with the German boy calling out "Gruss Gott" as the ship docked in Bremerhaven. In an interview by Elizabeth Janeway for the New York *Times Book Review* of April 1, 1962, Miss Porter explained the new structure: "The movement of the ship, forward, the movement of the waves, the movement of the passengers as they walk about the decks, all these got into the structure of the book. It moves in all these ways."

Until Miss Porter's journal entries made during the trip and later, her letter to Miss Gordon, and other documents concerning the composition are published, one must rely on Miss Porter's memory. Miss Janeway, for instance, assumed that La Condesa was fictional, but Miss Porter assured her such a person was aboard the ship she had sailed on. Eventually, when more is known of Miss Porter's life, it will be possible to identify people and character traits with more certainty. Now, however, one can only speculate; but there is, for example, reason to believe that Hart Crane, one of her acquaintances in Mexico not long before his suicide, is portrayed in the novel. Miss Porter seems to apportion certain of Crane's characteristics among three of her fictional men: the boorish Denny; Echegaray, the woodcarver whose knife is taken from him, thereby depriving him of his ability to express himself artistically; and Baumgartner, the alcoholic lawyer who threatens suicide by jumping from the ship.

Crane excitedly wrote friends on March 30, 1931, that he would soon sail for Mexico where he would establish himself in the country after spending a week with his "old and wonderful friend, Katherine Anne Porter,"[1] who was also awarded a Guggenheim grant that year. During the voyage, Crane spent hours talking to Dr. Hans Zinsser, the Harvard bacteriologist then on his way to Mexico with "a half dozen rats in the hold loaded with the deadly typhus."[2]

The night the ship sailed from Havana, Crane, who had been drinking heavily, came upon the bacteriologist who was dropping overboard a parcel wrapped in paper. The package broke open when it hit the water, and Crane saw two white rats struggling in the water and knew they were the typhus-infected specimens Dr. Zinsser was taking to Mexico for his experiments. Crane was, Philip Horton says, "seized by the drunken fantasy that his friend was diabolically poisoning the harbor of Havana, and began to shout frenzied warnings of the danger at the top of his voice."[3] Dr. Zinsser in *As I Remember Him* says that Crane spoke as if "scanning lines from his Bridge poem:—

> The Doctor has thrown rats into the harbor of Havana.
> The Doctor has thrown typhus rats into the water.
> There will be typhus in Havana.
> The Doctor has thrown rats into the harbor.[4]

Crane finally had to be confined to his cabin for the night. Miss Porter must have known of this rat incident, either from hearing about it from Crane or from reading Horton's biography of Crane when it appeared in 1937, for she contributed to it a long account of her relations with Crane.

The scene in *Ship of Fools* describing the drowning of Echegaray (which means, appropriately, Casanova) while rescuing the fat bulldog Bébé, deliberately thrown overboard by Ric and Rac, may well be indebted to Crane's observing of Dr. Zinsser casting the rats overboard. The drunken Denny who had been stalking the prostitute Pastora saw a "long dark bundle"—almost the same expression used by Horton—strike the water; then Ric and Rac ran by; Denny was then aware of another bundle hitting the water and the cries from steerage. Greatly agitated, Denny began to cry; and, in his drunkenness, he was almost as emotional as Crane was upon seeing the rats struggling in the water.

Other characteristics of Crane are seemingly transferred to Echegaray, the Jesus-like Basque. From bits of wood in his bundle he carved small animals (perhaps cranes?) to sell to first-class passengers. After his knife—and thus his hope—was taken from him, he sat crying, just as Crane, his artistic powers declining, often cried. Miss Porter leaves him a shadowy figure, and provides multiple answers to explain his rescue of Bébé: a completely disinterested act on the part of the Basque (even his nationality reminds one of Crane, who wore a Basque jersey); or, as the priest thinks, "a blamable disregard for his life"; or the hope of reward or a heroes' welcome; or a longing for death—suicide without the stigma associated with self-destruction. These multiple choices proposed by various characters in the novel parallel fairly closely the speculations on the causes and meaning of Crane's suicide, which included his disavowal of a world gone mad; his psychic, sexual malaise; his attempt to find mystical union with the universe.[5]

Crane joined Miss Porter in Mixcoac, a native suburb, but Miss Porter soon regretted inviting him to be her house guest, Horton reports, "for Crane, caught in the quickening constrictions of his fate . . . was fast becoming an insupportable companion."[6] When Miss Porter reached the end of her endurance, Horton says, and "persuaded him to find a home of his own, he rented the adjoining building, which, unfortunately for her, was vacant. . . ."[7] This first rupture in the friendship of the two writers was apparently more painful than Horton suggests, for Crane sent this message to her on April 28: "HAVE GONE TO THE MANCERA [a local hotel] UNTIL THE FIRST. EXCUSE MY WAKEFULNESS PLEASE. P.S. NO. HAVEN'T BEEN BUSY WITH 'LOVERS.' JUST YEOWLS AND FLEAS. LYSOL ISN'T NECESSARY IN THE BATHTUB. HAVEN'T GOT 'ANYTHING' YET."[8] This angry P.S. is echoed in *Ship of Fools*: Denny's cabin mate—David, who is Jenny's lover—is a fanatic about germs and constantly cleans the wash basin with something Denny thinks is carbolic acid. David was outraged to see Denny take a sponge bath, the body hair sticking to the side of the lavatory, and vowed to wash the bowl with disinfectant as soon as the Texan left the room. In an earlier printed version which appeared in *Harper's Magazine* of November, 1950, Miss Porter used the word *lysol*.

After Crane wrote abject notes begging forgiveness, the two writers again went on seeing each other. Horton indicates that the midnight brawls with his homosexual partners continued, but Horton says it was not the violence or the sordid sexual adventures which disturbed Miss Porter; it was rather "the terrible spectacle of a great talent, an essentially noble spirit, caught in the grip of a slow, inexorable disintegration."[9]

The final break was, for Crane, unexpected. In a long letter of explanation and self-justification, Crane told Lorna Dietz that he found Miss Porter's disposition quite different from what it was in New York. He admitted that he said outrageous things to her when he was drunk, but everything had been going smoothly before he invited her to dinner. He made extensive preparations for the meal, liberally sampling the tequila all the time. Miss Porter did not come to dinner; Crane roared into town, drank more, and later that night quarreled with Miss Porter at her gate. He recalled saying to her: " 'Katherine Anne, I have my opinion of you.' I was furious, of course, and I still have no reason for doubting that——[Miss Porter's companion] simply devised that insult deliberately."[10] He did not see her again, and she did not answer his letter of apology.

In her own carefully controlled recollections of this event, Miss Porter does not mention the missed dinner party at all but does describe the scene at the gate: Crane called her to pay his taxi fare; she says he claimed never to remember events when he was drunk but always sent money around the next day for the taxi fare. He wanted to come in, but she was "tired to death" and "at the end" of her patience and told him to go home; she continued:

> It was then that he broke into the monotonous obsessed dull obscenity which was the only language he knew after reaching a certain point of drunkenness, but this time he cursed things and elements as well as human beings. His voice at these times . . . stunned the ears and shocked the nerves and caused the heart to contract. In this voice and with words so foul there is no question of repeating them, he cursed separately and by name the moon, and its light: the heliotrope, the heaven-tree, the sweet-by-night, the star jessamine, and their perfumes. He cursed the air we breathed together, the pool of water with its two small ducks huddled at the edge, and the vines on the wall and house. But those were not the things he hated. He did not even hate us, for we were nothing to him. He hated and feared himself.[11]

Denny, the Texan, endowed with many of Crane's boisterous, vulgar characteristics, is brutally assaulted by Mrs. Treadwell the night of the dinner given by the Spanish dancers. Denny, after trailing the prostitute Pastora for days, hoping to avail himself of her services free or cheaply, was determined to have her that night. Drunkenly stumbling after her, he mistakenly stopped in front of Mrs. Treadwell's door (an approximation of Miss Porter's gate), yelling out "thick-tongued descriptions of the Gothic excesses he intended to commit upon Pastora's person, of which rape would be the merest preliminary"(464). Mrs. Treadwell (somewhat tipsy herself) had just painted on a face something like Pastora's; her assumed face seemed to reveal "something sinister in the depths of her character" (462). When she flung open the door, Denny grabbed her, saying, "Come out here, you whore" (464). Although she told him he was mistaken, he was too drunk to see that the painted face was merely a mask; she knocked him to the floor, struck him with her fist, and then pounded his face with the sharp heel of her shoe.

When she learned the next morning that the story was out that Pastora had attacked Denny with an ice pick, she laughed with great pleasure. She made no attempt to make amends to her victim; and, as fitting for such a self-isolated character, when leaving the ship at Gijón, she sat in the boat which carried the passengers to shore with her back toward the *Vera*, and therefore toward truth.

Although Miss Porter makes changes in the actual events at the gate in order to fit the incident into the fictional narrative, the scene is remarkably the same—with the addition of Mrs. Treadwell's violent retribution, which is taken against the errant, vulgar, brutal male only when she is masked.

Miss Porter also incorporates some of Crane's moods into her characterization of Herr Baumgartner, who has failed as a lawyer because of excessive drinking. On his tenth wedding anniversary, he quarreled with his wife and threatened to jump from the ship. His wife's reaction was similar to Miss Porter's nonchalance when Crane threatened to jump from the roof: "Oh don't," Miss Porter said, "It's not high enough and you'll only hurt yourself." Crane laughed and came down.[12] "Yes," Frau Baumgartner said to her husband, "you will make a big disturbance and be rescued like Bébé." When her husband replied that the Basque had been drowned, she replied, "You make me sick!" (453-54).

As he stood at the rail considering jumping, Herr Baumgartner conjured up a vision of his wife rushing to him, crying out, Joycean fashion, "Oh nonono, waitwait my love forgive me!" (454). In his self pity, he blamed Mrs. Treadwell, then passing by, for her indifference to his suffering. Actually, after she passed him and he had "turned a face of despair towards them, almost an appeal for help" (459-60), Mrs. Treadwell said to her companion, "He seems awfully sick somehow, perhaps dying" (460). His malaise, annoying though it was to those about him, was a sickness fully as acute as Crane's. His self-pity, too, was akin to Crane's; for, returning to his cabin, Herr Baumgartner cried out that his wife was knitting when he was about to destroy himself.

These three fictional characters are not Crane—they have been given some of Crane's characteristics or they perform acts which Miss Porter connected with Crane. The Crane affair, unpleasant as it must have been to her, had ample opportunity to enter her subconscious mind, to be transformed into art in a process she has described: "Now and again thousands of memories converge, harmonize, arrange themselves around a... coherent form, and I write a story."[13]

In *Ship of Fools* Miss Porter expresses—if these speculations connecting the relationship between her and Hart Crane with the novel are correct—a sharply ambivalent attitude toward the poet. Jenny, one of Miss Porter's major spokesmen, says on the morning of Echegaray's funeral: "Just think of him being left there all by himself" (324). But at the funeral, Jenny thought the whole scene "unreal, a pantomime [;] there was nothing that had ever been alive in the dark swaddle of canvas; and even as she wondered at her callousness, she felt her eyes filling with perfectly meaningless tears, tears for nothing at all, that would change nothing, that would not ease the pain of her emptiness; and through a mist she saw the canvas leap outward and strike the water" (328).

IV   *The Novel*

While the voyage to Europe was still clearly in mind, Miss Porter read in 1932, Sebastian Brant's *Das Narrenschiff* (1494). When she began planning the novel, she took, as she says, "this simple almost universal image of the ship of this world on its voyage to eternity." Brant's influence on the novel is much more pronounced than most critics, Mark Schorer excepted, have seen. Edwin H. Zeydel wrote of Brant,

> Brant was a man of deep religious convictions and of stern morality, even to the point of prudishness. His motives were of the highest. He wanted to elevate his generation, and dreamed too of improving its political condition through moral regeneration. He was a typical fifteenth-century savant.... Yet he was also nervous and irritable, positive and dogmatic, a carping satirist of the very follies of which he himself may often have been guilty. His tendency to seek weaknesses and flaws in others was congenital. His morality was philistine.[14]

Brant satirized the foibles and weaknesses of men, but as Henry Charles Lea wrote in the *Cambridge Modern History*, "the important feature of the work is the deep moral earnestness which pervades its jest and satire; man is exhorted never to lose sight of his salvation, and the future life is represented as the goal to which his efforts are to be directed."[15]

Miss Porter has retained much of the moral earnestness and the satiric thrusts of Brant, and she has also made special use not only of his ship image but also of the deadly sins. The sins against society including injustice, dishonesty, and uncharitableness; the sins of the church and the clergy, ill-advised prayers, irreverence in church, clerical excesses; the sins of lawyers, doctors, patients, bad women, beggars; the sins at the carnival, to name only some of the categories, are also abundant on Miss Porter's ship. Unlike Brant, Miss Porter presents developed characters instead of abstractions.

The allegory of good and evil is implicit in Miss Porter's version, but she has made the meaning more clear by using as a focal point the rise of the fascists in the 1930's, and the worldwide calamity which resulted from the mass movements led by Hitler, Mussolini, and Franco. She catalogued in detail the inertia and political naïveté among most of the Americans and Europeans on the *Vera*: the anti-Negro, anti-Mexican sentiments of the Texan Denny, attitudes still prevalent long after Nazism and fascism were officially dispelled in Germany and Italy; the Spanish dancers, prostitutes, pimps, criminals, managing to terrify the whole ship and to survive and even thrive; the Fatherland consciousness, the pig-headedness, the anti-Semitism, the self-pity, the cruelty of the Germans, based on Miss Porter's personal observations, both on the ship bound for Europe in 1931 and in Germany itself. Miss Porter incorporates virtually all of Brant's fools into her own political parable and sober warning.

One of the most brilliant qualities of the novel is the deft handling of point of view, which constantly shifts from character to character. As a result of the shifts, the reader sees characters and events from multiple angles of vision; and he begins to understand the complexity of the characters and the events. No one observer has the "truth"; no one observer is Miss Porter's spokesman. Mrs. Treadwell's bruised arm, for example, resulted from a beggar's pinch; but, when Dr. Schumann saw it, he thought it was from an amorous pinch. Time and time again, interpretations which seemed logical to those making the judgments are proved wrong.

The opening section, the first part of the Embarkation section with the rubric from Baudelaire—"*Quand partons-nous vers le bonheur?*" ("When shall we set out toward happiness") which is used ironically—is a sustained mood piece, a near-perfect introduction to the action and events which are to follow. Veracruz is described with overwhelmingly realistic details, and by implication Miss Porter extends her Veracruz to include all commercial cities and her passengers to include all the people of the world. Veracruz was a "little purgatory between land and sea" (3), and the reader soon learns that the embarking passengers were to leave one purgatory for another on ship, for another at their port of destination. At first, the sights and sounds, the local color, are stronger than the passengers themselves. The capitalistic-proletariat *leitmotif* which runs through the novel is introduced early: the Mexican capitalists were bloodthirsty, unfeeling, confident they would last a while longer. The proletariat were sometimes innocent victims (as was the boy killed in the bungled bombing), exploited, mistreated, treated no better than cattle, as were the hundreds of Spaniards put in steerage. Class and social differences are evident throughout the novel, not only in first class itself, with its own bitter divisions, but between first class and steerage.

One of the most horror provoking bits of local color, the maimed beggar, is found in Brant. As Zeydel rendered the passage:

> To beg some men will always choose,
> Though they could work if but they would,
> They're young and strong, their health is good,
> Save that their back they'll not incline,
> These sluggards have a corpse's spine.
> Their children in their youth they train
> To profit well by beggar's gain,
> To learn the cries—a mumper's token—,
> Or else they'd have their bones all broken
> Or so be maimed with welt and bruise
> That they would scream from sheer abuse.

In Miss Porter's version, the beggar, who had been deformed by a master, appeared on the terrace in Veracruz every morning (just as the clowns and dwarfs in "The Circus" appeared in the circus tent every day). Partially blind, and dumb, he crawled along the sidewalk like a dog, "wagging his hideous shock head from side to side slowly in unbearable suffering. The men at the table glanced at him as if he were a dog too repulsive even to kick..." (4-5). Miss Porter used, as she often does, animal imagery to describe man; but, in this instance, we see an example of her concreteness as opposed to Brant's abstraction, and her version of the perfidy of beggars surpasses Brant in horror, setting, and tone.

The travelers straggled into the plaza and the restaurant slowly, and the reader sees them as the travelers themselves would view a group awaiting passage, or as the Mexican waiters see them. The insolent waiters stared at the motley assortment of travelers, at the fat couple with the fat bulldog Bébé. The night before, the clerk had told the woman, "No, Señora, even if this is only Mexico still we do not allow dogs in our rooms" (12). The humor and gentle irony of this passage is followed by a comic, mock-heroic description: "The ridiculous woman had kissed the beast on his wet nose before turning him over to the boy who tied him up in the kitchen patio for the night. Bébé the bulldog had borne his ordeal with the mournful silence of his heroic breed, and held no grudges against anybody" (12). Miss Porter's complete control of language, which perhaps derives partially from Sterne, is beautifully demonstrated here.

The horror of the death of the young Indian boy, killed by mistake in the bombing of the Swedish Embassy, made almost no impression on the travelers; and they were equally unconcerned about the Indian arrested by the police. Herr Rieber predicted the man would be shot, but his pre-Nazi mentality is not to be trusted—he wanted inferior races shot, or put into gas ovens. The bored reactions of the Mexicans discussing the bombing become a parable for man's reactions to violence and symbolic of the madness which the world was headed for in less than ten years.

Miss Porter at first gives surface impressions of the Germans, Americans, the Swede, the three Swiss, and the Spanish dancers and their two children. Some of the members begin to appear in focus: the Huttens, parents of Bébé; Mrs. Treadwell, who has a large bruise on her arm because she had refused alms to a beggar. Miss Porter emphasizes not only the beastliness of the beggar woman but also the aloofness and alienation of the woman who refused to give money to her. In groups, couples, and one by one, Miss Porter introduces her cast of characters; then we see many of them again through the eyes of the ship's doctor, Dr. Schumann, who, from his first description, seems suspect, because of two dueling scars on his face. The standard reaction of slight repulsion is proved wrong, however, for Dr. Schumann is not a bigoted fraternity man, but a professional man of talent, a professional observer with a clinical eye but with human compassion, a representative of what was good in a Germany of the past; but he is dying of a heart disease, just as the "good" Germany was dying.

The doctor soon wandered away, and a Mexican bride and groom become the center of attention. They are almost completely shrouded during the whole trip, and they and the Mexican woman, baby, and maid seem less fools than the other passengers, perhaps because they are almost completely outside the action. The fat Mexican in the cherry-colored shirt, a figure remarkably similar to Braggioni in "Flowering Judas," also seems shadowy at first; and, instead of being menacing, he is faintly humorous. His collar button, like that of Fat Stuff in the comic strip "Smilin' Jack," flew off; when he was ordered off the first-class deck, he protested, but went below, a mock revolutionary.

With their luggage in their cabins, the passengers begin to take on identity. Love, sex, and jealousy are introduced in the first pairings on the *Vera*: the pre-Nazi, pig-like Rieber, and his Lizzi, and Arne Hansen, a sex-ridden Swede. The feud of the two men over Lizzi lasted the entire trip, coming to a climax the night of the captain's ball. The Spanish dancers, without their pimps, were ogled by Denny, the sex-crazed, perenially unsuccessful Texan. He shared a cabin with Herr Glocken (whose name suggests the Hunchback of Notre Dame) and David Scott, lover of the American girl Jenny Brown, who had caused such a scandal in Veracruz by appearing in slacks. David and Jenny were constantly at each other, consuming each other in their love-hate relationship. One of the peculiarities of Miss Porter's examination of love and sex at this time is her ignoring of the theme of homosexuality.

Frau Rittersdorf, disappointed because she had not made a profitable marriage in Mexico, had in pique turned against the dark races; to assure proper respect from her cabin mate, she had sent herself flowers, with appropriate messages, signing one with the name of a dead baron. The reader's initial contempt for this vain woman is tempered with her diary entry on Jenny and David. She found the names musical but sentimental: "Jenny Angel—the real name is, I suppose, Jane, Johanna Engel it would be, and much better, in the German—and David Darling. The latter is a common surname as well as a usual term of affection among Americans, I believe; much less among the frozen English naturally, though it does seem to be a corruption of the word *Dear,* Dearling, the diminutive; this would sound as if pronounced Darling, since the English have a slovenly way of speaking certain words . . ." (84). The entry is comic not only because Frau Rittersdorf has parodied, unconsciously, much German philological pedantry, but also because it is clear that Miss Porter is not taking herself too seriously. It is well known that Miss Porter kept a journal on the voyage, and she is, in effect, casting doubts on the validity of the observations and pretensions of diary keepers.

The Huttens' fat bulldog Bébé is comic and ludicrous, a perfect illustration of Dr. Johnson's famous definition: "Bulldog . . . A dog of particular form, remarkable for his courage. He is used in baiting the bull; and his species is so peculiar to Britain, that they are said to degenerate when they are carried to other countries." Bébé had degenerated, but through no fault of his own. Overfed and overprotected, he was constantly seasick. He is one of Miss Porter's few sympathetic characters on board the ship, and one feels pity for this bull baiter who makes no protest when Ric and Rac toss him overboard.

Ric and Rac have been widely misinterpreted as pure incarnations of evil. Six-year-old twin children of Lola, one of the members of the Zarzuela company, their life was spent among whores and pimps. They were outcasts patterning their lives on a cartoon popular in Mexico: the wire-haired terriers in the comic strip "made fools of even the cleverest human beings in every situation, made life a raging curse for everyone near them, got their own way invariably by a wicked trick, and always escaped without a blow" (17). They outwitted even their parents by throwing La Condesa's pearls overboard. In some ways they seem in their perversity and in their intransigence, outrageous caricatures of Miss Porter's—and Everyman's—own characteristics as a child; more importantly, they have been shaped by the Zarzuela company and by society, which supported the newspaper cartoons. Miss Porter did not set out—in the characters of Ric and Rac or in some of the pre-Franco Spaniards or pre-Nazi Germans, or in the pre-Little Rock Southerners—to define the exact nature of good and evil. Nor does she see the possibility of the redemption of man. Echegaray, the Jesus-like character, sacrificed himself to rescue Bébé—a parody of Jesus dying for mankind—but nobody understood, nobody cared, least of all the priests.

It is in Part II, "Kein Haus, keine Heimat . . ." (no house, no home), in which we see the travelers, alienated, without permanent house or home, revealing much of their true nature. Three women are of special interest; all three are, in one way or another, spokesmen for Miss Porter. Jenny, the young artist, seems partially autobiographic: she was from the South, from a large family which had disapproved of her wanting to be an artist; she had been much interested in liberal causes and believed in direct participation in political protest. Unfortunately, Jenny had allowed David to influence her work, and she no longer used the bright colors in her paintings that she had once employed. She is only slightly disillusioned; she is another Miranda still capable of seeing the world (if not always her lover) with perception. The love-hate relationship of Jenny and David is one of the major themes of the novel.

Mrs. Treadwell, the 45-46-year-old divorcee, wanted to withdraw from all contact but was inevitably drawn into the life of Freytag, the handsome businessman who both loved and hated his Jewish wife. Mrs. Treadwell, a secret alcoholic, unwittingly revealed that Freytag's wife was Jewish (she is, then, a traitor just as Laura in "Flowering Judas" was) and brought about his downfall among the Germans at the captain's table. In her alienation, Mrs. Treadwell is much like the unnamed narrator in "Hacienda." Her assault upon Denny comes at the end of the captain's dinner and is her vengeance taken upon the errant male.

La Condesa is also a spokesman for Miss Porter; a slightly

grotesque, once-beautiful woman constantly in need of sex, she accepted the company of the Cuban medical students; in need of drugs, she received them from Dr. Schumann. But, with all of her foibles and large and small human failings, she is much more than a decayed member of the aristocracy. She is grief-stricken Greek driven to the point of madness by the uncertainty of the fate of her sons. Her emotions are larger than life; but, in a world of dislocation, her sufferings are understandable and telling. Too, she alone could understand and not condemn the incestuous relationship of Ric and Rac, an act which horrified the doctor and the young ship's officer. Lastly, she was capable of love; and the love affair with the doctor, though doomed, is one of the most admirable (which is to say, less animalistic) examples of love in the novel.

The Germans, products of an authoritarian culture, are author-itarian, autocratic, sentimental. Except for Herr Rieber and the captain, they are not in themselves vicious but they can be led to cruelty. The willingness to send Freytag away from the captain's table because of his Jewish wife is a brilliant parable of the rise of Nazism and anti-Semitism. The pride in race, the self-satisfaction of the remaining Germans, the failure of the intellectual Dr. Schumann to defend Freytag—all are realistic and at the same time symbolic. Miss Porter has extended her allegory to the universal human condition; she shows the racism of Denny and of Löwenthal. When the members of the Zarzuela company stole the prizes for the Captain's Gala, virtually every-one in first class saw what they were doing; but nobody did anything about it.

Löwenthal has many of the despicable traits of the Germans, for Miss Porter has not presented a romantically conceived stage Jew. He is self-satisfied, a shrewd businessman selling religious goods and bragging of his work, just as Chaucer's Pardoner did. "There's money it it" (96), Löwenthal said; it had nothing at all to do with religion, it was just business.

One of the most pathetic of the Germans is Johann Graf, the handsome young boy taking his dying uncle to Germany for a last visit. The grotesque old uncle, a religious fanatic, thinks he has the power of healing; but he is too unobservant to see the problems of his nephew. Johann, crazed by sex, has no money to pay Concha, who suggests that the boy kill the old man;

for, though drawn to Johann, she still insists that he buy her love. The agony of Johann, his taking the money instead of killing his uncle, and his initiation into sexual activity are followed by attempts to be kind to the old man, attempts which fail because the boy is misunderstood just as Stephen was in "The Downward Path to Wisdom."

Also of special interest is the fate of the agitator in the red shirt. At the funeral service, he often belched loudly and "made the sign of the Cross with his thumb on the end of his nose" (326). The devout in steerage, angered, fell upon him; and the fat revolutionary was struck a strong blow on the head. The reactions to the attack are brilliantly analyzed, from Jenny's impotent tears, to Hansen's cry "Kill your enemies, not your friends" (328), to the captain's disgust, "Let them decimate each other if they like, but not on my ship" (344). When the revolutionist left the ship, he was dazed and had to be helped. Dr. Schumann thought he would recover and get into more trouble, but the account as parable is of the weakening of the revolutionary movement.

The huge cast of characters introduced in the first section are seen intimately and distantly, wrongly and obliquely in this long second section. The third section begins with a quotation from St. Paul: "For here have we no continuing city..."

The central scene is the Captain's Gala. The parallel to Brant is explicit: In the section on Carnival Fools, he wrote that revelers often pretended to mask their identity in order to commit immoral acts. At Miss Porter's carnival-like dinner, all semblance of morality was swept away. Hiding behind a mask, as we have seen previously, Mrs. Treadwell attacked Denny; but Mrs. Treadwell was not alone. The thieving, amoral Spanish dancers proposed, symbolically, a pact with Germany; Herr Baumgartner goose-stepped and was followed by goose-stepping children—a modern Pied Piper leading the children to destruction. The pathetic Herr Glocken with his pink necktie inscribed "Girls, Follow Me!" (419); Hansen's attack on Herr Rieber; the ribald Cucaracha song; the drunkenness of David, Denny, Baumgartner, Jenny; the dishonest drawing for prizes were only a few of the actions of the fools, actions which stripped from them the last vestiges of civilization.

Johann, who relieved his sexual desire, would not lie, would not say he loved Concha. The Mexican couple, in their happiness, wanted to die young or live forever; naïve they may have been, but they were not a part of the headlong plunge into barbarism.

The horrible events of the night meant nothing to the passengers. The injured were treated; the gulled did nothing about their betrayal; Mrs. Treadwell turned her back on the events; David and Jenny went on quarreling; the Germans went on making their plans for re-entering the Fatherland. The professor spoke for them the cliché: "At last we are nearing home, and we are, after all, all good Germans together. Let us thank God for his blessings" (493).

Miss Porter has, by the end of the novel, explored attitudes toward life and death, love and sex, religion and religiosity, love and hate, racism and politics; she has presented the deadly sins in old forms and in new guises. She has drawn upon all her years of experience and upon all her artistic powers, upon the artistic methods which she learned from Joyce, James, Eliot, Brant, and others. Harry J. Mooney, Jr., argues that the novel is too restricted because Miss Porter portrays a hate-driven world "little susceptible to the claims of reason and intelligence." Mooney isolates what he thinks is a major defect of the novel: "the possibility of human nobility" is absent. One could argue, however, with equal validity, that had Miss Porter emphasized "human nobility" or even the possibility of human nobility, she would not have given a true picture of the 1930's or of much of man's experience in the twentieth century. Miss Porter sees the possibility offered by the wood carver; but, because of the *human condition,* his act does not bring salvation, is not even a worthy example. Miss Porter has written in *Ship of Fools* a gigantic novel, subtle and forceful, naturalistic and symbolic, allegorical and political.

CHAPTER 6

The Essays

M ISS PORTER'S essays and reviews are much more difficult to evaluate than her fiction. As she explained in the Foreword to *The Days Before,* her essays—unlike the fiction—were requested by publishers who set space and subject limitations. Although she often wrote under great pressure, she expressed her ideas as clearly as possible and regarded the articles which she chose to reprint as a journal of her "thinking and feeling." The articles and reviews were avowedly written for money, but they were not, she insisted, "the other half of a double life. . . . The two ways of working helped and supported each other: I needed both."

Many of the book reviews—published primarily in the New York *Times Book Review,* the New York *Herald-Tribune Books, The Nation,* and *The New Republic*—were ephemeral and are now of little interest, even to Miss Porter's most devoted readers, and Miss Porter wisely did not collect them. But, for those interested, Edward Schwartz's excellent bibliography gives a thorough listing through 1952 of articles and reviews.

I *"Critical"*

Miss Porter's selection of articles for republication is generally commendable, for under three headings—"Critical," "Personal and Particular," and "Mexican"—she has preserved the best of her completed, non-fiction writing. One notices immediately, however, that her style is at times far inferior to her fictional style; the essay on James called "The Days Before," written first in 1943 and revised in 1952, is an example. Although the article is a long one, it is little more than an effective retelling of some of the highlights of James's life. It is a pedestrian piece, especially since she is an admirer of James and much influenced by his technique.

In "1939: The Situation in American Writing," Miss Porter had declared herself as "James-minded" rather than "Whitman-minded," and no one who has read her works would want to deny this obvious and beneficial influence. Perhaps writing on James frightened her, made her lose, temporarily, the light touch. A few phrases in "The Days Before" are recognizably hers, and certainly the conclusion is magnificently stated: "no man has ever seen any relations concluded. Maybe that is why art is so endlessly satisfactory: the artist can choose his relations, and 'draw, by a geometry of his own, the circle within which they shall happily *appear* to do so.' While accomplishing this, one has the illusion that destiny is not absolute, it can be arranged, temporized with, persuaded, a little here and there. And once the circle is truly drawn around its contents, it too becomes truth." Miss Porter goes beyond James and approaches both a personal and a philosophical statement on art itself.

"On a Criticism of Thomas Hardy" (1940) is a much better essay than "The Days Before" because Miss Porter brandished her biting and heavy satire in deprecating Hardy's critics. She saved her heaviest salvoes for T. S. Eliot, who after his conversion, she wrote, was writing literary judgments which "assumed the tone of lay sermons...." Miss Porter proceeded to quote from Mr. Eliot's panegyric on Hardy and then craftily and wittily demolished the argument. The defense of the novelist and the iconoclastic attack on the pontifications of the poet are sustained throughout the essay. Miss Porter in her rôle as Eliot-slayer is remarkably effective.

In "Everybody Is a Real One" (1927), Miss Porter had her first say on Gertrude Stein; and she was, if baffled at times, sympathetic, a young writer in the presence of one of the great influences of modern literature. One year later, Miss Porter, like many another of Miss Stein's supporters, had drawn away. Miss Porter, obviously never a strong supporter, in "Second Wind" furnished a wicked and telling satire on Miss Stein, mocking the mannerisms thoroughly.

Almost twenty years later, Miss Porter returned to Miss Stein in "The Wooden Umbrella" (1947), put her parody aside, but completely decimated Miss Stein and her writing. With a vibrant, smooth style, Miss Porter reviewed the artistic and social career of Miss Stein, and found it lacking. Miss Porter wrote page after page of brilliantly fashioned sentences, each one sentencing, by comparison, Miss Stein to artistic oblivion.

"Reflections on Willa Cather" (1952) is a delicately phrased appreciation of a major American writer, one who influenced Miss Porter strongly. The essay is particularly important because she explains in it not only what Miss Cather meant to her but also some of her own background-reading in twentieth-century literature. When Miss Porter began to read Miss Cather, she also read James, Yeats, Conrad, Stein (but *Tender Buttons* was symptomatic of much modern literature which hid lack of feeling behind "disordered syntax" or "tricky techniques"), and Joyce. But after Miss Porter had savored the new literature and art and music, she could see, finally, her ties to the world and to the artistic creed of Miss Cather. The essay tells almost as much about Miss Porter as it does about Miss Cather and is, above all, a brilliant defense of the provincial in literature, a quality shared by these two women writers.

"It Is Hard to Stand in the Middle" (1950) is a well-reasoned, artistic defense of Ezra Pound. She begins by acknowledging James, Joyce, Yeats, Eliot, and Pound as the writers who educated her: "The beginning artist is educated by whoever helps him to learn how to work his own vein, who helps him to fix his standards,' and who gives him courage." Miss Porter rightly emphasized Pound's incessant labors for other writers, but she also saw that he was opinionated and had a gift for making enemies as well as friends. Whenever Pound ventured beyond art and poetry, he was liable to the grossest mistakes; she saw that he was not only anti-Semitic but anti-Christian. She concluded, optimistically: "Most of the things and the kind of people he fought are still sitting about running things, fat and smug. That is true. And a great many of the talents he tried to foster came to nothing. Fighting the dark is a very unfashionable occupation now; but it is not altogether dead, and will survive and live again largely because of his life and example."

"The Art of Katherine Mansfield" (1937), though shorter than the appreciation of Willa Cather, is important as a guide to Miss

Porter's indebtedness but is an all-too-brief comment on Miss Mansfield's best stories. The essay is slighter than the Pound one, for example, and seemingly only partially because of space limitations. Miss Porter obviously admired Miss Mansfield, but the appreciation lacks flair and the usual Porter grace and style.

"Orpheus in Purgatory" (1950), a brief, impressionistic essay on Rilke, is interesting gossip, but the book-review editor apparently did not allow Miss Porter scope to present Rilke more completely. The essay is a disappointing one and probably should not have been republished. Similarly, "The Laughing Heat of the Sun" (1949) is an appreciation of Edith Sitwell's work. The second paragraph captures the mood and approach: "Miss Sitwell's early work belonged to youth—it had the challenging note of natural arrogance, it was boldly experimental, inventive from a sense of adventure, full of high spirits and curiosity as to how many liberties the language would suffer to be taken without hitting back. There was sometimes also a certain artifice, the dew upon the rose turned out to be a crystal bead on a mother-of-pearl petal. Yet it was the work of a deft artificer, and a most ornamental rose, meant to amuse and charm, never intended to be mistaken for a natural flower." Although Miss Porter writes delightfully of the poet, it is obvious that she does not find Miss Sitwell a modern master.

"Eudora Welty and 'A Curtain of Green'" (1941) is much warmer, much more enthusiastic than the notice of Miss Sitwell. Without being pedantic, Miss Porter sketched in essential facts from Miss Welty's biography, her intellectual and artistic development, and the themes of her stories. Miss Porter, the established artist, was not condescending in her introduction; and her appreciation was amazingly perceptive: she found that Miss Welty was not writing "false or labored" stories, that she was making a direct approach to her material, and that "there is even in the smallest story a sense of power in reserve which makes me believe firmly that, splendid beginning that this is, it is only the beginning."

Of the next three appreciations, of Ford Madox Ford, Virginia Woolf, and E. M. Forster, the one on Mrs. Woolf is of particular interest. Miss Porter speaks of Mrs. Woolf as "one of the writers who touched the real life of my mind and feeling very deeply; I had from that book [*The Voyage Out*] the same sense of some mysterious revelation of truth I had got in earliest youth from Laurence Sterne. . . ." Miss Porter was drawn to Ford, however, not because each of his sixty books was good but because he made each work "as good as he was capable of making it at that moment" and because his life work and his vocation were the same. Poverty-stricken and neglected, Ford went on indomitably with his work, and Miss Porter obviously saw a parallel to her own career. The slight essay on Forster begins with a personal reminiscence and ends with a personal appreciation of his "admirable style." Since she is known as a stylist herself, her comment is of special interest: "his own style [is] spare, unportentous but serious . . . fearless but not aggressive." She admired his *Two Cheers for Democracy* which was "an extension and enlargement of his thought, a record of the life and feelings of an artist who has been in himself an example of all he has defended from the first: the arts as a civilizing force, civilization itself as the true right aim of the human spirit," and his belief in the importance of love "not in the mass, not between nations . . . but between one person and another."

II *"Personal and Particular"*

Some of the essays in "Personal and Particular" are closely connected with writings in the critical section. In "Three Statements about Writing" Miss Porter stated her preference for James over Whitman, but she went on significantly: "Neither James nor Whitman is more relevant to the present and future of American literature than, say, Hawthorne or Melville, Stephen Crane or Emily Dickinson; or for that matter, any other first-rank poet or novelist or critic of any time or country. James or Whitman? The young writer will only confuse himself, neglect the natural sources of his education as artist, cramp the growth of his sympathies, by lining up in such a scrimmage." Answering a question on the motivation of her writing, she said, "My whole attempt has been to discover and understand human motives, human feelings, to make a distillation of what human relations and experiences my mind has been able to absorb."

For some reason, Miss Porter also reprinted the 1940 Introduction to *Flowering Judas*, which appears in the Modern Library edition. She explains that she had not written more because "I was not one of those who could flourish in the conditions of the past two decades. They are fragments," she said of her stories, "of a much larger plan which I am still engaged in carrying out, and they are what I was then able to achieve in the way of order and form and statement in a period of grotesque dislocations in a whole society when the world was heaving in the sickness of a millennial change." She defended the artist, who represents "the substance of faith and the only reality." Miss Porter's note that the Introduction was written seven days after the fall of France helps clarify the tone of this brief but eloquent introduction.

"Transplanted Writers" (1942) is primarily interesting because she wrote of the evil at work during World War II as "the oldest evil with a new name," and she agreed with E. M. Forster that only art and religion offered possibilities for order. Such was also her conclusion to her essay on James, and much of her fiction is an attempt to impose order on the chaos of human existence.

"No Plot, My Dear, No Story" (1942) is at the same time a satire on slick-magazine fiction, on writing courses with all the answers on plots, and an extremely personal defense of the short story of theme. Unfortunately, the satiric passages are more crude than is usual with Miss Porter; and, since her examples are so obviously fictional, one almost forgets that she has in mind *The Saturday Evening Post, Mademoiselle,* and all the rest.

Although Miss Porter announced her non-commercialism in "No Plot, My Dear, No Story," she wrote an article for *Flair* on "The Flower of Flowers" (1950) which was embarrassingly commercial. Immediately following this excursion into the lore of roses, Miss Porter reprinted "Portrait: Old South" (1944), which is one of her most touching accounts of Grandmother Porter and the culture into which Miss Porter was born. This essay, which is indispensable for any interpretation of the Miranda stories, is discussed in Chapter 3.

But then Miss Porter turned to a travel piece, "Audubon's Happy Land" (1939), a description of a tour of plantation homes near St. Francisville, Louisiana. The essay is not quite social history, not quite *Holiday Magazine* local color; and the nostalgia for the Old South is somehow not quite in focus. Equally inconsequential is "A House of My Own" (1941) and

Miss Porter on love and marriage in "The Necessary Enemy" (1948) and in "Marriage Is Belonging" (1951).

"The Future Is Now" (1950) is a more important statement on how to live in the shadow of the atomic bomb, on how to avoid despair. She concluded, rather midway between optimism and pessimism: "And yet it may be that what we have is a world not on the verge of flying apart, but an uncreated one—still in shapeless fragments waiting to be put together properly. I imagine that when we want something better, we may have it: at perhaps no greater price than we have already paid for the worse." She argues that if dropping the bomb was immoral, then making it was, too: the first criminal "then was the man who first struck fire from flint, for from that moment we have been coming steadily to this day and this weapon and this use of it. What would you have advised instead? That the human race should have gone on sitting in caves gnawing raw meat and beating each other over the head with the bones?"

III *"Mexican"*

The Mexican Section is of particular interest because it contains many fugitive pieces and the excellent introduction to her translation of Lizárdi's *The Itching Parrot* (1941). The biographical and critical study is elegantly written, with keen insights into late eighteenth- and nineteenth-century Mexican life. Miss Porter obviously knew her Mexican history, and this sense of the Mexican past is reflected in the early Mexican stories.

"Why I Write About Mexico" (1923) and "The Mexican Trinity" (1921) were discussed in Chapter 2, but "Leaving the Petate" (1931) is serious social criticism, masked with a humorous account of Indian servants. Instead of the bitter irony of "Hacienda" or *Ship of Fools,* Miss Porter uses gentle humor in this essay to analyze the Mexican social revolution. She said of her maid, who was putting aside the straw mat Indians usually slept on for a brass bed and respectability, when she was marrying a barber: "Her children will be added to the next generation of good little conservative right-minded dull people, like Enrique, or, with Eufemia's fighting spirit, they may become *mestizo* revolutionaries, and keep up the work of saving the Indian."

"La Conquistadora" (1926) is the retelling of the story of Rosalie Evans, a Texas-born widow of an Englishman, who recaptured her Mexican hacienda after it had been seized during the Madero revolution. Mrs. Evans, who had no understanding of the reasons of the Mexican Revolution, saw the history of the country in terms of the economic effect upon herself. After six years, she was ambushed. Miss Porter's final judgment was, "As a human being she was avaricious, with an extraordinary hardness of heart and ruthlessness of will; and she died in a grotesque cause."

"The Charmed Life" (1942) is an account of Miss Porter's friendship with Mr. Niven, the prototype of Givens in "María Concepción." The essay is evocative, but Miss Porter knew him too short a time to write with any depth about his character; as a result, he seems much more fragmentary than his fictional counterpart in "María Concepción."

"Quetzalcoatl" (1926) was a review of D. H. Lawrence's *The Plumed Serpent*. Lawrence, she said, had risen above his usual confusion and with poetic power had found "a mystical truth." She praised the evocative powers of his language, but she found at the center of the rhetoric and the sexual emotions "a sick void." And she concluded with a harsh but valid judgment: "When you have read this book read *Sons and Lovers* again. You will realize the catastrophe that has overtaken Lawrence."

IV *Two Uncollected Essays*

Miss Porter's views on Lawrence continued to harden and in 1959 she published "A Wreath for the Gamekeeper," a slashing attack against Lawrence and *Lady Chatterley's Lover*: "Why should I defend a worthless book just because it has a few dirty words in it? Let it disappear of itself and the sooner the better." Miss Porter found Lawrence a badly flawed artist, who either did not know what he was doing, or, if he did, was pretending to be doing something else. She chillingly summed up the theme of the novel as "the activities of the rutting season between two rather dull persons. . . ."

Her objection to Lawrence's language was pointedly stated: "I would not object, then, to D. H. Lawrence's obscenity if it were really that. I object to his misuse and perversions of obscenity, his wrong headed denial of its true nature and meaning. Instead of writing straight, healthy obscenity, he makes it sickly sentimental, embarrassingly so, and I find that obscene sentimentality is as hard to bear as any other kind. I object to this pious attempt to purify and canonise obscenity, to castrate the Roaring Boy, to take the low comedy out of sex. We cannot and should not try to hallow these words because they are not hallowed and were never meant to be." This passage is also useful in understanding Miss Porter's decidedly unsentimental treatment of sex in *Ship of Fools*. The essay is a classic, of its kind, more devastating than Dwight Macdonald's "By Cozzens Possessed."

Also in the category of Miss Porter's finest work is "'Noon Wine': The Sources," discussed previously. It traces the beginnings of characters, moods, and ideas which were finally transformed into the short novel. The essay is one of the finest of its kind, equal in every respect to James's prefaces; it can be appreciated for its own beauty and purity of language, quite apart from the short novel which it explains.

V *Cotton Mather*

The biography of Cotton Mather has been promised for over thirty years; and, since publication of *Ship of Fools*, Miss Porter has again been speaking of its publication. The few chapters which have appeared are even more promising than the fragments of *Ship of Fools* which appeared for many years in many magazines before publication in book form. We know the outlines of Cotton Mather's life; we may not have read all 444 items which he published, but we know him as an incredibly pious, stuttering, priggish young divinity student, as a witch hunter, a religious and political reactionary, and as a neurotic, sexually possessed Puritan divine. It is certainly true, as the editors of *The Literature of the United States* have said, that to understand him is to "explore the intellectual labyrinth of provincial America in the period between 1680 and 1728."

The chapters on Mather published by Miss Porter, then, have a context in American intellectual and religious history which is particularly fascinating. We do not need to seek a design as we did with the chapters from *Ship of Fools*. Too, unlike many of the

essays in *The Days Before* which were hurriedly done, the Cotton
Mather study has been leisurely worked on, the prose is as
finely textured as the best of her fiction, and the irony comes
naturally from the subject. This passage from "Affectation of
Praehiminincies" is an example of the style and irony of the
chapters which have been published:

> When he was three years old, he could read and spell, and
> his serious education began in the free school of Mr. Benjamin
> Thompson. Family legend contends that he was an apostle
> from the first, and stammer or no, he began at once to lead
> his schoolmates in prayer. At playtime he preached little
> sermons to them. The feebler wits of the school listened and
> were impressed, but sturdier spirits made fun of him, poked
> him and pinched him when the master was not by, and gave
> him the joy of suffering for his principles. Increase Mather
> liked to believe that his child was a saint at three years, and
> resented the treatment he received. He encouraged him in his
> unutterable priggishness, and soothed his vanity by explaining
> that persecution was the fate of good souls in a wicked world.

Miss Porter has a decided point of view, as this quotation
shows; and the biography promises to be more readable, more
honest than Lytton Strachey's biographical sketches. In addition,
Miss Porter has mastered completely the complex social, economic, and political problems of Mather's New England. The
terrible childhood of this terrible man, as well as the theological
and political battles of Increase Mather, are treated brilliantly
in the opening section.

In "A Goat for Azazel, (A. D. 1688)" Miss Porter presents
Mather as a witch hunter. Beginning with the possessed Goodwin children, Miss Porter clearly states a rational explanation
for the children's activities: they gained immediate attention,
were freed from their usual duties, could terrorize their parents
and exhibit themselves freely in an age which did not allow
any of these under normal circumstances. Worn out by their
acrobatics, the children would recover at night, eat heartily, and
sleep well before beginning all over again the next day. Then
Martha, fourteen years old, named the witch who possessed
her—Bridget Glover, a Catholic and an Irishwoman. Martha
had quarreled with Bridget's daughter, and Bridget was known

to be peculiar; when she was under stress, she lapsed into
Gaelic. Miss Porter's psychological probing of witchcraft is as
clear and as pointed as Arthur Miller's in *The Crucible*. Bridget
was, of course, hanged; but from the scaffold she predicted the
children would not receive relief since "others besides herself
had a hand in their sufferings." Miss Porter then remarked,
pertinently, "This was truth with unconscious irony. The ones
who had a hand in it published this statement at once, and
the Goodwin children fell into fresh complexities of torment."

Mr. Mather took Martha into his own house for observation;
and, whenever she fell into a fit, he could always make it pass by
stroking her throat. Miss Porter paints scenes of high comedy,
of bigotry, stupidity, duplicity, constantly stressing the psychological motivations: "For several months the Mather household
lived in tumult. Martha was the center of attraction, and she
repaid the attentions given her. A dozen times a day Mather
forced her to her knees to pray with her. She clapped her hands
over her ears and declared They were raising such a clamor
she could not hear a word. At times she walked with a heavy
limp, and she explained that They had clamped Bridget Glover's
chain on her leg. Mather would strike at the invisible chain and
it would fall away."

The rather timid contemporary excuse justifying the Reverend
Mr. Mather because other scholars believed in witchcraft will not
do, as this section shows. Had he not been a vain, self-centered,
sexually possessed man, he would have seen through Martha's
guise immediately. But Miss Porter allows us to see the scene
with all of its comic and terrible connotations. Miss Porter's
long account of the possessed Martha ends by explaining the title
and its application to Mather: "A passage from the witchcraft
section of his *Magnalia Christi Americana* is poetically applicable
to Bridget Glover's part in the Goodwin episode: 'When two
goats were offered unto the Lord (and only unto the Lord) we
read that one of them was to fall by lot to Azazel . . . it is no
other than the name of the Devil himself.'"

In "A Bright Particular Faith, A.D. 1700" Miss Porter used
the final illness of Mrs. Abigail Mather as a vantage point to
study the Reverend Mr. Mather's faith and morals. Following a
miscarriage, Mrs. Mather became desperately ill, but Mr. Mather,
in his *Diary* for June 6, 1702, wrote, "And on this Day, I mett

with wonderful Things. In the Forenoon, while I was at Prayer, with my dying Wife, in her Chamber, pleading the Sacrifice of my Lord Jesus Christ, for my Family, I began to feel the blessed Breezes of a *Particular Faith,* blowing from Heaven upon my mind; I began to see that my dear Consort should be restor'd unto me, by the same good Hand that bestow'd her at first upon me. And I resolv'd, that in a Way of Gratitude, I would study certain particular Methods, to recommend the use of the Lord Jesus Christ, as a *Family-Sacrifice,* in the Faith of His People. . . . I then went unto my Consort, and assured her, that she should live yett awhile."

Miss Porter's version utilizes all the ironies involved, using a flowing, never obtrusive style: "Later he returned to his study, and this particular faith was intensified by intimate assurances from Heaven that she would not die at present. He resolved, in writing, that if the Lord would spare his Good Thing he would be wise and chaste and holy in his conversation with her ever afterward. He hastened to tell Abigail the happy news that she was to be spared to him. She grew worse immediately."

Miss Porter wrote at length on the effects on his faith of Abigail's approaching death—his final belief that Death and Abigail had been united against him. He turned against his prayers for her and her family and resolved to marry again. The Mather biography promises to be a major work, perhaps equaling in literary qualities many of Miss Porter's best stories.

Edward Greenfield Schwartz in "The Way of Dissent: Katherine Anne Porter's Critical Position" brought together her scattered statements on art, esthetics, religion, chiefly from essays in *The Days Before;* and he attempted to distill from them Miss Porter's critical position. While there are obvious dangers in drawing together statements made over a long period of time and out of essays not always personal, Professor Schwartz has judiciously shown the nature of her thinking on artistic questions. His conclusion is incontrovertible: Miss Porter's quest "for moral definition led not to philosophy or religion but to art. She thus became the inheritor of a great tradition— the tradition of dissent and inquiry, of selfless devotion to the search for meaning and order in the world of fiction."

CHAPTER 7

Conclusion

MISS PORTER considers herself an artist: "I'm one of the few living people not afraid to pronounce that word," she said in 1958. "Even Hemingway and Faulkner don't say they are artists. I've often wondered why people interested in the mind and human heart have been intimidated. . . ."[1] For over forty years now, she has gone her own artistic way, and in her writing she has continually told a "straight story." When she began writing, stories had to be written according to "a slick formula that was being used by the magazines and being practiced with great skill by a handfull of craftsmen."[2] Miss Porter "wrote honest," and honest stories then and now do not often have widespread appeal. For over thirty years she has had a superb critical reputation, but until *Ship of Fools* appeared in 1962 she was never widely read.

Over the last four decades, Miss Porter's short stories have been marked by a mastery of technique, by honesty, and by a desire to explore the human heart and mind and society itself, without lapsing into popular clichés. No matter whether she has written about Mexicans, Texans, Irishmen, or Germans, one feels that she knows the people and their backgrounds perfectly; she has lived and relived the experiences and emotions so thoroughly that she has often written her stories and short novels in a matter of hours or days.

She had developed her fictional techniques by the time she published her first story, and technically she has shown little improvement because she began with a fully developed, mature form. "Holiday," one of her most recent stories, is a brilliant technical and psychological achievement, but it is not better written nor more meaningful than "María Concepción."

Miss Porter is a conscious artist, in the tradition of James and Joyce; she has known what she wanted to say and what mood she wished to create. She has destroyed much of what she has written because it did not meet her high standards. Just how demanding her standards have been is best illustrated by a careful reading of the slim volume of her work. One finds story after story of near perfection. Some stories such as "Flowering Judas" and "Noon Wine" have been widely anthologized and analyzed, but they are not superior to "He," "The Downward Path to Wisdom," or "The Circus," to name only a few.

Her themes have been important; James William Johnson suggests that they are "of the individual within his heritage," of "cultural displacement," of unhappy marriages and the accompanying self-delusion, of "the death of love," of "man's slavery to his own nature and subjugation to a human fate which dooms him to suffering and disappointment." One might retitle, reorder, expand or contract these categories; but, as stated by Professor Johnson, they succinctly indicate some of her main concerns.

She has constantly dealt with the chaos of the universe and with the forces within man and within society which have led to man's alienation. Her probings of the human condition are deeply personal and yet, because of the constant play of irony in everything she writes, impersonal also.

Her often and justly praised style is never mannered, is perfectly adaptable to her material, and is characterized by clarity. She has consciously avoided stylistic characteristics or peculiarities which would make it instantly recognizable. No skeleton keys are needed to unlock her stories or her style. She learned from Sterne, Mrs. Woolf, Joyce, James, and others; but she set out not to imitate them but to write simply and clearly, flowingly and flawlessly. She used her admirable style to create characters of complexity, characters which grip the imagination: María Concepción, Braggioni, Miranda, Stephen, Homer T. Hatch, Papa Müller, to name only a few. She also re-created with authority the social backgrounds of Mexico, of turn-of-the-century Texas, of Denver during wartime, of immigrant Irish in the slums.

Her rank as a major short story writer is not in question. Her stories should be compared, Robert Penn Warren correctly says, with those of Joyce, Hemingway, Katherine Mansfield, and Sherwood Anderson. Her essays and book reviews, because of the press of time, are generally not so carefully fashioned as the short stories; but " 'Noon Wine': The Sources" is an exception. It is as beautifully written and as meaningful as the story itself. The biography of Cotton Mather also promises to be a major work.

The delay of *Ship of Fools* was gossiped about for years, and after its unexpected (to Miss Porter) success—to some critics Book-of-the-Month Club sponsorship led immediately to author damnation—there were innuendoes that she had abandoned her high artistic standards in order to gain popular success. All the evidence is against this, I think. She says she wrote the book she set out to write, and *Ship of Fools* does not pander to middle-class taste or morality. The theme of the novel could hardly give aid and comfort to any class or nationality. The novel is more than a series of vignettes, for it is carefully planned, each sketch integrated into the allegorical, political, social, and psychological themes. It is a candid, frank, realistic, symbolic story which brings together all of Miss Porter's knowledge of the world and its people; and in it she demonstrates that her artistic powers have not diminished.

Miss Porter is correct in her self-estimation: she is an artist.

Notes and References

Chapter One

1. Philadelphia *Evening Bulletin*, October 27, 1961, p. 19.
2. "Notes on Writing," *New Directions, 1940* (Norfolk, Conn., 1940), p. 203.
3. Donald Stalling, *Katherine Anne Porter: Life and the Literary Mirror*. Unpublished M.A. thesis, Texas Christian University, 1951.
4. Philadelphia *Evening Bulletin*, October 27, 1961, p. 19.
5. *Twentieth Century Authors* (New York, 1942), pp. 1118-19.
6. Archer Winsten, "Presenting the Portrait of an Artist," New York *Post*, May 6, 1937, p. 17.
7. *Ibid.*
8. Glenway Wescott, *Images of Truth* (New York, 1962), p. 29.
9. See essays on individual authors in *The Days Before*.
10. Paul Crume, "Pale Horse, Pale Rider," *Southwest Review*, XXV (January, 1940), 214.
11. Undated clippings from *The Critic*, probably September or October 1917.
12. Kathryn Adams Sexton, *Katherine Anne Porter's Years in Denver*. Unpublished M.A. thesis, University of Colorado, 1961.
13. Crume, *op. cit.*, p. 214.
14. *Bulletin of the New York Public Library*, LVII (May, 1953), 219.
15. Philip Horton, *Hart Crane: The Life of an American Poet* (New York, 1957), pp. 283-85; for Miss Porter's letter about Crane see pages 285-87; for an interpretation of the Crane-Porter relationship, see Chapter V.
16. Brom Weber, editor, *The Letters of Hart Crane* (New York, 1952), p. 378.
17. New York *Herald-Tribune*, April 6, 1940, p. 9.
18. *Newsweek* (International edition), July 31, 1961, p. 39; *Time* (International edition), July 28, 1961, p. 65.
19. *Current Biography* (New York, 1940), p. 658.
20. Robert Penn Warren, "Irony with a Center: Katherine Anne Porter," in *Selected Essays* (New York, 1958), p. 137.

Chapter Two

1. Charles A. Allen, "Katherine Anne Porter: Psychology as Art," *Southwest Review*, XLI (Summer, 1956), 225; James Hafley, "'María Concepción': Life among the Ruins," *Four Quarters*, XII

(November, 1962), 11-17; James William Johnson, "Another Look at Katherine Anne Porter," *Virginia Quarterly Review*, XXXVI (Autumn, 1960), 605, 608, 611; Harry J. Mooney, Jr., *The Fiction and Criticism of Katherine Anne Porter* (Pittsburgh, 1957), pp. 48-49; Ray B. West, Jr., *Katherine Anne Porter* (Minneapolis, 1963), p. 8.

2. "María Concepción" may well have begun as one of the anecdotes of her Mexican friend, Niven.

3. Johnson, *op. cit.*, p. 607.

4. This may well be an allusion to Henry James's *In the Cage*.

5. Allen, *op. cit.*, pp. 227-29; Johnson, *op. cit.*, pp. 603-4, 611; Mooney, *op. cit.*, pp. 47-48; Katherine Anne Porter, "Flowering Judas" in Whit Burnett, ed., *This Is My Best* (New York, 1942), pp. 539-40; Robert Penn Warren, "Irony with a Center: Katherine Anne Porter," in *Selected Essays*, 140-43, originally appeared in *Kenyon Review* in 1942; Ray B. West, Jr., "Theme through Symbol," in *The Art of Modern Fiction* (New York, 1949), pp. 287-92; West, *Katherine Anne Porter*, pp. 9-12.

6. See Whit Burnett, *op. cit.*, pp. 539-40.

7. *Recent Southern Fiction: A Panel Discussion* (Macon, Ga., 1960), p. 12.

8. Allen, *op. cit.*, pp. 229-30; Johnson, *op. cit.*, p. 606; Mooney, *op. cit.*, pp. 39-40; this section first appeared, in a slightly different form, in *Four Quarters*, XII (November, 1962), 24-29.

9. Howard Baker, "Some Notes on New Fiction," quoted in Edward Schwartz, "Katherine Anne Porter: A Critical Bibliography," *Bulletin of the New York Public Library*, 57 (May, 1953), 241.

10. Mooney, *op. cit.*, p. 39.

11. Marie Seton, *Sergei M. Eisenstein* (London, 1952), pp. 195-96.

12. *Ibid.*, pp. 515-16.

13. S. M. Eisenstein, *Que Viva Mexico!* (London, 1951), pp. 47-62.

14. Johnson, *op. cit.*, pp. 604, 611; Mooney, *op. cit.*, p. 51; Marjorie Ryan, "*Dubliners* and the Stories of Katherine Anne Porter," *American Literature*, XXI (January, 1960), 470-71; Ray B. West, Jr., *op. cit.*, p. 9.

15. James Ruoff and Del Smith, "Katherine Anne Porter on *Ship of Fools*," *College English*, XXIV (February, 1963), 397.

Chapter Three

1. James William Johnson, "Another Look at Katherine Anne Porter," *Virginia Quarterly Review*, XXXVI (Autumn, 1960), 602; Charles Kaplan, "True Witness: Katherine Anne Porter," *Colorado*

Quarterly, VII (Winter, 1959), 621; Harry J. Mooney, Jr., *The Fiction and Criticism of Katherine Anne Porter*, pp. 16-17; Ray B. West, Jr., *Katherine Anne Porter*, pp. 24-25.

2. Johnson, *op. cit.*, p. 602; Kaplan, *op. cit.*, pp. 322-23; Mooney, *op. cit.*, p. 16; West, *op. cit.*, p. 25.

3. John V. Hagopian, *Insight I* (Frankfurt, 1962), pp. 212-15; Johnson, *op. cit.*, *pp.* 602, 610; Kaplan, *op. cit.*, pp. 321-22; Mooney, *op. cit.*, pp. 17-19; Ray B. West, Jr., *op. cit.*, pp. 26-27.

4. Johnson, *op. cit.*, p. 602; Charles Kaplan, *op. cit.*, p. 324; Harry J. Mooney, Jr., *op. cit.*, p. 16; West, *Katherine Anne Porter*, pp. 25-26.

5. Johnson, *op. cit.*, pp. 605, 609, 611.

6. James William Johnson first noticed Miss Porter's use of Blake.

7. Johnson, *op. cit.*, p. 605, 609-10; Kaplan, *op. cit.*, pp. 323-24; Harry J. Mooney, Jr., *op. cit.*, p. 19; S. H. Poss, "Variations on a Theme in Four Stories of Katherine Anne Porter," *Twentieth Century Literature*, IV (April-July, 1958), 21-24; Edward G. Schwartz, "The Fictions of Memory," *Southwest Review*, XLV (Winter, 1960), 205-6; West, *Katherine Anne Porter*, pp. 27-28.

8. Schwartz in "The Fictions of Memory," a most perceptive essay, points out Huck Finn's similar feelings.

9. Johnson, *op. cit.*, pp. 605, 609-11; Kaplan, *op. cit.*, pp. 324-25; Mooney, *op. cit.*, pp. 19-20; Schwartz, *op. cit.*, pp. 214-15; West, "Katherine Anne Porter and 'Historic Memory,'" pp. 278-79; see also West, *Katherine Anne Porter*, pp. 28-29.

10. Charles A. Allen, "The Nouvelles of Katherine Anne Porter," *University of Kansas City Review*, XXIX' (December, 1962), 88-90; Cleanth Brooks and Robert Penn Warren, *Understanding Fiction* (New York, 1943), pp. 529-34; Kaplan, *op. cit.*, pp. 325-27; Harry J. Mooney, Jr., *op. cit.*, pp. 20-25; Poss, *op. cit.*, pp. 24-25; Schwartz, *op. cit.*, pp. 206-8; Robert Penn Warren, "Irony with a Center: Katherine Anne Porter," *Selected Essays*, pp. 149-54; West, "Katherine Anne Porter and 'Historic Memory,'" pp. 285-89; also see West, *Katherine Anne Porter*, pp. 15-20.

11. Allen, "The Nouvelles of Katherine Anne Porter," pp. 90-92; Johnson, *op. cit.*, pp. 604, 609, 611; Mooney, *op. cit.*, pp. 25-33; Poss, *op. cit.*, pp. 23-25; West, *Katherine Anne Porter*, pp. 20-22; Sarah Youngblood, "Structure and Imagery in Katherine Anne Porter's 'Pale Horse, Pale Rider,'" *Modern Fiction Studies*, V (Winter, 1959), 344-52.

12. Denver *Post*, March 22, 1956. Quoted in Kathryn Adams Sexton, "Katherine Anne Porter's Years in Denver," unpublished M.A. thesis, University of Colorado, 1961, pp. 84-85.

Chapter Four

1. James William Johnson, "Another Look at Katherine Anne Porter," *Virginia Quarterly Review*, XXXVI (Autumn, 1960), 611; Harry J. Mooney, Jr., *The Fiction and Criticism of Katherine Anne Porter*, p. 48.

2. Charles A. Allen, "The Nouvelles of Katherine Anne Porter," *University of Kansas City Review*, XXIX (December, 1962), 87-88; Johnson, *op. cit.*, p. 605; Mooney, *op. cit.*, pp. 40-44; Marvin Pierce, "Point of View: Katherine Anne Porter's *Noon Wine*," *The Ohio University Review*, III (1961), 95-113; Katherine Anne Porter, "'Noon Wine': The Sources," *Yale Review*, XLVI (September, 1956), 22-39; Robert Penn Warren, "Irony with a Center: Katherine Anne Porter," *Selected Essays*, pp. 143-48; Glenway Wescott, *Images of Truth*, pp. 39-43; Ray B. West, Jr., "Katherine Anne Porter and 'Historic Memory,'" *Southern Renascence*, pp. 281-82; West, *Katherine Anne Porter*, pp. 12-13.

3. Charles A. Allen, "Katherine Anne Porter: Psychology as Art," *Southwest Review*, XLI (Summer, 1956), 225-27; John V. Hagopian, *Insight I*, pp. 208-11; Johnson, *op. cit.*, pp. 605, 611; Mooney, *op. cit.*, pp. 49-50; West, *Katherine Anne Porter*, p. 9.

4. Johnson, *op. cit.*, pp. 605, 611; Mooney, *op. cit.*, p. 51.

5. Johnson, *op. cit.*, pp. 604, 611; Mooney, *op. cit.*, p. 48; Marjorie Ryan, "*Dubliners* and the Stories of Katherine Anne Porter," *American Literature*, XXXI (January, 1960), 471.

6. Allen, "Katherine Anne Porter: Psychology as Art," pp. 223-24; Johnson, *op. cit.*, p. 610; Mooney, *op. cit.*, pp. 51-54; Ryan, *op. cit.*, pp. 467-68; West, *Katherine Anne Porter*, p. 29.

7. Johnson, *op. cit.*, pp. 605, 611; Mooney, *op. cit.*, p. 51.

8. Allen, "Katherine Anne Porter: Psychology as Art," pp. 224-25; Johnson, *op. cit.*, pp. 604, 611; Mooney, *op. cit.*, pp. 44-46; Ryan, *op. cit.*, pp. 468-69; Warren, *op. cit.*, pp. 148-49; Brother Joseph Wiesenfarth, "Illusion and Allusion: Reflections in 'The Cracked Looking-Glass,'" *Four Quarters*, XII (November, 1962), 30-37; West, *Katherine Anne Porter*, p. 9.

9. Johnson, *op. cit.*, pp. 604, 611; Mooney, *op. cit.*, p. 50; Ryan, *op. cit.*, pp. 465-67; West, *Katherine Anne Porter*, pp. 29-30.

10. Hagopian, *op. cit.*, pp. 216-19; Richard Poirier, *Prize Stories 1962: The O. Henry Awards* (New York, 1963), pp. vii-x.

11. Allen, "The Nouvelles of Katherine Anne Porter," pp. 92-93; Johnson, *op. cit.*, pp. 603-4, 607, 611; Mooney, *op. cit.*, pp. 35-39; Ryan, *op. cit.*, pp. 472-73; West, *Katherine Anne Porter*, pp. 30-32;

Edmund Wilson, "Katherine Anne Porter," in *Classics and Commercials* (New York, 1950), pp. 220-21; Vernon Young, "The Art of Katherine Anne Porter," in *American Thought—1947*, pp. 234-37.

Chapter Five

1. Brom Weber, ed., *The Letters of Hart Crane* (New York, 1952), p. 367. All subsequent references cited as *Letters*.
2. *Ibid.*, p. 368.
3. Philip Horton, *Hart Crane: The Life of an American Poet* (New York, 1957), pp. 280-81.
4. Hans Zinsser, *As I Remember Him* (Boston, 1946), p. 337.
5. Horton, *op. cit.*, pp. 303-4.
6. *Ibid.*, p. 284.
7. *Ibid.*, p. 285; Horton unfortunately does not include footnotes or bibliography, and his sources are not readily identifiable; perhaps much of this section in his book was based on what Miss Porter told him.
8. *Letters*, p. 369.
9. Horton, *op. cit.*, p. 285.
10. *Letters*, pp. 377-78.
11. Horton, *op. cit.*, p. 286.
12. *Ibid.*, p. 287.
13. "Notes on Writing," *New Directions, 1940* (Norfolk, Conn., 1940), p. 203.
14. Sebastian Brant, *The Ship of Fools*, translated by Edwin H. Zeydel (New York, 1962), p. 7.
15. Quoted in Fr. Aurelius Pompen, *The English Versions of The Ship of Fools* (London, 1925), p. 1; Fr. Pompen's study is of immense help to anyone interested in Brant's satire.

Chapter Seven

1. *Texas Observer*, October 31, 1958, p. 6.
2. *Ibid.*

Selected Bibliography

PRIMARY SOURCES

1. Collected Works

The Days Before. New York: Harcourt, Brace and Co., 1952. Contents: "The Days Before," "On a Criticism of Thomas Hardy," "Gertrude Stein: Three Views," "Reflections on Willa Cather," " 'It Is Hard to Stand in the Middle,' " "The Art of Katherine Mansfield," "Orpheus in Purgatory," " 'The Laughing Heat of the Sun,' " "Eudora Welty and 'A Curtain of Green,' " "Homage to Ford Madox Ford," "Virginia Woolf," "E. M. Forster," "Three Statements about Writing," "No Plot, My Dear, No Story," "The Flower of Flowers," "Portrait: Old South," "Audubon's Happy Land," "A House of My Own," "The Necessary Enemy," " 'Marriage Is Belonging,' " "American Statement: 4 July 1942," "The Future Is Now," "Notes on the Life and Death of a Hero," "Why I Write About Mexico," "Leaving the Petate," "The Mexican Trinity," "La Conquistadora," "Quetzalcoatl," "The Charmed Life."

Flowering Judas and Other Stories. New York: The Modern Library, 1940. Contents: "María Concepción," "Magic," "Rope," "He," "Theft," "That Tree," "The Jilting of Granny Weatherall," "Flowering Judas," "The Cracked Looking-Glass," "Hacienda."

The Leaning Tower and Other Stories. New York: Harcourt, Brace and Co., 1944. Contents: "The Source," "The Witness," "The Circus," "The Old Order," "The Last Leaf," "The Grave," "The Downward Path to Wisdom," "A Day's Work," "The Leaning Tower."

Pale Horse, Pale Rider: Three Short Novels. New York: The Modern Library, 1949. Contents: "Old Mortality," "Noon Wine," "Pale Horse, Pale Rider."

Ship of Fools. Boston: Little, Brown and Co., 1962.

2. Selected listing of Uncollected Works

"The Adventures of Hadji: A Tale of a Turkish Coffee-House," retold by Katherine Anne Porter. *Asia,* XX (August 1920), 683-84. A battle-of-the-sexes story told in archaic language, but with some characteristic touches of irony. She has not collected this first published story of hers; the note on contributors is of interest: "She has written many ballet pantomimes and children's stories and has corresponded for Texas newspapers from the Mexican border."

For a *Biography of Cotton Mather:*
"Affectation of Praehiminincies," *Accent,* II (Spring 1942), 131-38; (Summer 1942), 226-32.

"A Bright Particular Faith A.D. 1700," *Hound and Horn*, VII (January, 1934), 246-57.

"A Goat for Azazel (A.D. 1688)," *Partisan Review*, VII (May-June, 1940), 188-99.

"The Fig Tree," *Harper's Magazine*, CCXX (June, 1960), 55-59.

"Holiday," *Atlantic Monthly*, CCVI (December, 1960), 44-56. Reprinted in *Prize Stories 1962: The O. Henry Awards*, with an introduction by Richard Poirier. Greenwich, Connecticut: Fawcett World Library, 1963.

"The Martyr," *The Century Magazine*, CVI (July, 1923), 410-13.

" 'Noon Wine': The Sources," *Yale Review*, XLVI (September, 1956), 22-39. Reprinted in Brooks and Warren, *Understanding Fiction,* Second Edition. New York: Appleton-Century-Crofts, Inc., pp. 610-20.

"Notes on Writing," *New Directions, 1940*. Norfolk, Connecticut: New Directions, 1940, pp. 195-204. Important journal entries from 1931-1936; enough to make all students wish to see a comprehensive edition from her journals.

"On First Meeting T. S. Eliot," *Shenandoah*, XII (Spring, 1961), 25-26. A splendid description of Eliot at a noisy cocktail party.

"Society Gossip of the Week" and "The Week at the Theaters," undated 1917 clippings from *The Critic*.

"Virgin Violeta," *The Century Magazine*, CIX (December, 1924), 261-68.

"Where Presidents Have No Friends," *The Century Magazine*, CIV (July, 1922), 373-84. Unfortunately not collected in *The Days Before*. An important article for understanding Miss Porter's views on Mexico in the early 1920's.

"A Wreath for the Gamekeeper," *Shenandoah*, XI (Autumn, 1959), 3-12; also appeared in *Encounter*, XIV (February, 1960), 69-77. See also note by Richard Aldington and letter by Richard Rees in the April, 1960, *Encounter*, pp. 51-54 and p. 87 and Miss Porter's reply to Mr. Aldington in the May issue, p. 85.

3. *Poetry* (see the Schwartz bibliography for a listing of Miss Porter's poetry). "My poem as I look at it this morning is not so good as I hoped. It began well and may end well, but there is a long way to go. Sometimes I have regretted destroying all that poetry I worked on for so many years, but now I believe I was right," Miss Porter wrote in her *Journal* in 1931. One regrets the destruction of Miss Porter's poetry in much the same way that one is sorry that Thoreau destroyed much of his poetry. Miss Porter's poetry, like Thoreau's, is not equal to her prose, but the few poems she has published do give us a record of her inner life.

SECONDARY SOURCES

1. Bibliography

SCHWARTZ, EDWARD. "Katherine Anne Porter: A Critical Bibliography." With an introduction by Robert Penn Warren. *Bulletin of The New York Public Library,* LVII (May, 1953), 211-47. Indispensable. An admirable guide, through 1952, of Miss Porter's writings, with sections on "Books," "First Appearance of Stories and Poems (and some Important Reprints)," "Essays and Comments," "Book Reviews," and "Work in Progress." Also included is a valuable section on criticism of Miss Porter's works, divided into two parts: "General" and "About Individual Works."

SYLVESTER, WILLIAM A. "Selected and Critical Bibliography of the Uncollected Works of Katherine Anne Porter," *Bulletin of Bibliography,* XIX (January, 1947), 36.

THURSTON, JARVIS, O. B. EMERSON, CARL HARTMAN, ELIZABETH V. WRIGHT. *Short Fiction Criticism.* Denver: Alan Swallow, 1960, pp. 176-80. A good guide to criticism of the individual stories.

WALKER, WARREN S. *Twentieth-Century Short Story Explication.* Hamden, Connecticut: The Shoe String Press, Inc., 1961, pp. 312-19. Somewhat more extensive than the Thurston listing.

WOODRESS, JAMES. *Dissertations in American Literature 1891-1955 with Supplement 1956-1961.* Durham: Duke University Press, 1962. For dissertations on Miss Porter, see pp. 37, 99.

2. Biography

AARON, DANIEL. *Writers on the Left.* New York: Harcourt, Brace & World, 1961. Quotes an article by Michael Gold which says that Miss Porter, Dos Passos, and others were arrested in Boston for picketing the State House during the Sacco-Vanzetti case. Valuable background material on the radical movement.

BLOCK, MAXINE. *Current Biography.* New York: The H. W. Wilson Co., 1940. An important biographical source.

JOSEPHSON, MATTHEW. *Life Among the Surrealists.* New York: Holt, Rinehart and Winston, 1962. Recollections of Miss Porter during the late 1920's after her return from Mexico.

KUNITZ, STANLEY J. and HOWARD HAYCRAFT. *Twentieth Century Authors.* New York: The H. W. Wilson Co., 1942. For additional biographical information, see *Twentieth Century Authors, First Supplement,* edited by Stanley J. Kunitz and Vineta Colby. New York: The H. W. Wilson Co., 1955.

SEXTON, KATHRYN ADAMS. *Katherine Anne Porter's Years in Denver.* Unpublished University of Colorado M.A. thesis, 1961. Includes source material on Miss Porter in Denver, the setting of "Pale

Horse, Pale Rider," and a listing of Miss Porter's signed newspaper articles.

STALLING, DONALD. *Katherine Anne Porter: Life and the Literary Mirror.* Unpublished Texas Christian University M.A. thesis, 1951. I am indebted to the Dean of the Graduate School of Texas Christian University for permission to examine and quote from this pioneering biographical study of Miss Porter. Mr. Stalling brought together material of utmost value for any biographical study of Miss Porter.

3. *Interviews*

"The Best Years," *Newsweek* (International Edition), July 31, 1961, p. 39. A prepublication interview, with information about *Ship of Fools.*

BODE, WINSTON. "Miss Porter on Writers and Writing," *Texas Observer,* October 31, 1958, pp. 6-7. Miss Porter being charming to a young writer turned interviewer. A stunning photograph of Miss Porter in floppy hat.

DOLBIER, MAURICE. "I've Had a Good Run for My Money," New York *Herald-Tribune Books,* April 1, 1962, pp. 3, 11. Personal history and an account of the writing of *Ship of Fools.*

"First Novel," *Time* (International Edition), July 28, 1961, p. 65. A prepublication interview. "Of the past, says Author Porter, peering through the wake of two decades: 'I've survived but I certainly haven't flourished. I think Hemingway beat me to it by about twenty paces. Honestly, I am so tired.' "

FOLEY, EILEEN. "Katherine Anne Porter Gets a Gift, Day of Her Own at LaSalle College," Philadelphia *Evening Bulletin,* October 27, 1961, p. 19. Miss Porter on writing and teaching of writing.

GIRSON, ROCHELLE. "The Author," *Saturday Review,* XLV (March 31, 1962), 15. Some incorrect biographical information, including the year of Miss Porter's birth, but with an important statement of Miss Porter's aim in the novel and a comment on modern-day Germans—"they are just as dangerous as they were"—which has been widely disputed in Germany.

"James: 'The Turn of the Screw.' A Radio Symposium," Katherine Anne Porter, Allen Tate, Mark Van Doren in *A Casebook on Henry James's "The Turn of the Screw."* New York: Thomas Y. Crowell Company, 1960, pp. 160-70. Reprinted from *The New Invitation to Learning.* Important statements from Miss Porter on the nature of evil.

JANEWAY, ELIZABETH. "For Katherine Anne Porter, 'Ship of Fools' Was a Lively Twenty-Two Year Voyage," New York *Times Book Review,* April 1, 1962, pp. 4-5. A detailed discussion of the writing of *Ship of Fools.* More family history.

Selected Bibliography

"Recent Southern Fiction: A Panel Discussion. Katherine Anne Porter, Flannery O'Connor, Caroline Gordon, Madison Jones, Louis D. Rubin, Jr., Moderator," Macon, Georgia: Wesleyan College, October 28, 1960. Miss Porter ranges from family history to original sin.

RUOFF, JAMES and DEL SMITH. "Katherine Anne Porter on *Ship of Fools*," *College English* XXIV (February 1963), 396-97. A basic statement on the background and meaning of the novel.

"Some Important Authors Speak for Themselves," New York *Herald-Tribune Books*, October 12, 1952, p. 8. Miss Porter's comments on her ballet and music study and her love of cats.

THOMPSON, BARBARA. "The Art of Fiction XXIX—Katherine Anne Porter: An Interview," *Paris Review*, No. 29 (Winter-Spring, 1963), pp. 87-114. The most extensive interview yet published; much family history and theorizing on writing. Reproduction of a manuscript page of *Ship of Fools*.

VAN GELDER, ROBERT. "Katherine Anne Porter at Work," *Writers and Writing*. New York: Charles Scribner's Sons, 1946. An important early interview, with information about her life and her method of working.

WINSTEN, ARCHER. "Presenting the Portrait of an Artist," New York *Post*, May 6, 1937, p. 17. An important early interview, with much material on family history and her theory and method of writing.

"Writing a Prize Story Is Easy—To Miss Porter," New York *Herald-Tribune*, April 6, 1940, p. 9. Early comments on *Promised Land*, an earlier title for *Ship of Fools*, plus comments on her strict rearing by a grandmother and her escape to the North, where women writers were not considered "depraved."

4. *Criticism of Stories*

(See Schwartz's bibliography for a more complete listing.)

ALLEN, CHARLES A. "Katherine Anne Porter: Psychology as Art," *Southwest Review*, XLI (Summer, 1956), 223-30. A valuable psychological examination of a few of the short stories; an especially perceptive treatment of "The Downward Path to Wisdom."

————. "The Nouvelles of Katherine Anne Porter," *The University of Kansas City Review*, XXIX (December, 1962), 87-93. A balanced study of the short novels; attempts to show Miss Porter's strengths and weaknesses as "artist, psychologist, and moralist."

BLAKE, WILLIAM. *Poetry and Prose of William Blake*. Edited by Geoffrey Keynes. London: The Nonesuch Press, 1927.

BURNETT, WHIT, ed. "Why She Selected Flowering Judas," *This Is My Best.* New York: The Dial Press, 1942.

COWSER, ROBERT G. "Porter's THE JILTING OF GRANNY WEATHER-ALL," *The Explicator,* XXI (December, 1962), No. 4. The two jiltings—secular and religious, the latter being more important.

CRUME, PAUL. "Pale Horse, Pale Rider," *Southwest Review,* XXV (January, 1940), 213-18. Not entirely reliable, as Schwartz points out in his bibliography, but the controversy over whether or not Miss Porter worked as a reporter on the Dallas *News* (reported as fact by Crume) is moot; Miss Porter has both admitted and denied that she worked for that paper.

EISENSTEIN, S. M. *Que Viva Mexico!* London: Vision Press, Ltd., 1951. Contains sketchy script for the movie which has its fictional counterpart in "Hacienda."

HAFLEY, JAMES. "'María Concepción': Life among the Ruins," *Four Quarters,* XII (November, 1962), 11-17. A new reading.

HAGOPIAN, JOHN V. "Katherine Anne Porter: Feeling, Form, and Truth," *Four Quarters,* XII (November, 1962), 1-10. A spirited reading, by a critic much influenced by Susanne Langer.

HAGOPIAN, JOHN V. and MARTIN DOLCH. *Insight I.* Frankfurt: Hirchgraben, 1962. Hagopian gives new critical analyses of "The Jilting of Granny Weatherall," "The Old Order," and "Holiday."

HENDRICK, GEORGE. "Katherine Anne Porter's 'Hacienda,'" *Four Quarters,* XII (November, 1962), 24-29. Republished, in slightly different form, in Chapter 2.

JOHNSON, JAMES WILLIAM. "Another Look at Katherine Anne Porter," *The Virginia Quarterly Review,* XXXVI (Autumn, 1960), 598-613. A classification of stories according to themes: "the individual within his heritage," "cultural displacement," unhappy marriages and accompanying self-delusion, "the death of love and the survival of individual integrity," "man's slavery to his own nature and subjugation to a human fate which dooms him to suffering and disappointment"; and "Hacienda" which stands alone.

KAPLAN, CHARLES. "True Witness: Katherine Anne Porter," *Colorado Quarterly,* VII (Winter, 1959), 319-27. A chronological reordering of the Miranda stories; especially pertinent remarks on "The Circus."

KIELY, ROBERT. "The Craft of Despondency—The Traditional Novelists," *Daedalus,* XCII (Spring, 1963), 220-37.

MARSHALL, MARGARET. "Writers in the Wilderness: Katherine Anne Porter," *The Nation,* CL (April 13, 1940), 473-75. A biographical essay, not entirely reliable, and a short appreciation of Miss Porter's stories.

Selected Bibliography

MOONEY, HARRY JOHN, JR. *The Fiction and Criticism of Katherine Anne Porter*. Pittsburgh: University of Pittsburgh Press, 1957. A revised edition with a chapter on *Ship of Fools* was published in 1962. This first monograph on Miss Porter is particularly good on political implications of her work.

NANCE, WILLIAM L., S.M. *Katherine Anne Porter & the Art of Rejection*. Chapel Hill: University of North Carolina Press, 1964. This study, which also contains a chapter on *Ship of Fools*, arrived too late for inclusion in my text. Brother Nance argues, "At the heart of Katherine Anne Porter's literary achievement lies a principle of rejection." For a criticism of his thesis and method, see Caroline Gordon, "Katherine Anne Porter and the ICM," *Harper's Magazine* CCXXIX (November 1964), 146-48.

O'CONNOR, WILLIAM VAN and EDWARD STONE. *A Casebook on Ezra Pound*. New York: Thomas Y. Crowell Co., 1959. Background material on Bollingen award to Pound. Miss Porter was a member of the committee which awarded the prize.

PIERCE, MARVIN. "Point of View: Katherine Anne Porter's *Noon Wine*," *The Ohio University Review*, III (1961), 95-113. A detailed investigation of point of view in the eight sections of the story.

POSS, S. H. "Variations on a Theme in Four Stories of Katherine Anne Porter," *Twentieth Century Literature*, IV (April-July, 1958), 21-29. An investigation of "the What Is Worth Belonging To theme" in "The Circus," "Old Mortality," "Pale Horse, Pale Rider," and "The Grave."

PRAGER, LEONARD. "Getting and Spending: Porter's 'Theft,' " *Perspective*, XI (Winter, 1960), 230-34. "The story's central irony is that 'Theft' comes principally through unwillingness to spend oneself."

RYAN, MARJORIE. "*Dubliners* and the Stories of Katherine Anne Porter," *American Literature*, XXXI (January, 1960), 464-73. An introduction to the difficult subject of Miss Porter's indebtedness to Joyce; unfortunately, the study is restricted to *Dubliners*, ignoring the other works of Joyce which were equally influential.

SCHWARTZ, EDWARD GREENFIELD. "The Fictions of Memory," *Southwest Review*, XLV (Summer, 1960), 204-15. An excellent study of Miranda and the Miranda stories. Especially good on the conflict of the old and new order and the use of memory.

————. "The Way of Dissent: Katherine Anne Porter's Critical Position," *Western Humanities Review*, VIII (Spring, 1954), 119-30. A thorough study.

SETON, MARIE. *Sergei M. Eisenstein*. London: The Bodley Head, 1952. Background information on "Hacienda."

SINCLAIR, UPTON. *The Autobiography of Upton Sinclair.* New York: Harcourt, Brace & World, Inc., 1962, pp. 262-67. Background information on Eisenstein and the filming of *Que Viva Mexico!*

STEIN, WILLIAM BYSSHE. " 'Theft': Porter's Politics of Modern Love," *Perspective,* XI (Winter, 1960), 223-28. In "Theft," Miss Porter "correlates [the] corruption of the instinct and spirit with the disintegration of traditional religious authority."

WARREN, ROBERT PENN. "Irony with a Center: Katherine Anne Porter," *Selected Essays.* New York: Random House, 1958. Undoubtedly the most influential article on Miss Porter. Her irony implies "a refusal to accept the formula, the ready-made solution, the hand-me-down morality, the word for the spirit."

WEST, RAY B., JR. "Katherine Anne Porter: Symbol and Theme in 'Flowering Judas,' " *Accent,* VII (Spring, 1947), 182-87. Reprinted in *The Art of Modern Fiction.* New York: Rinehart and Co., Inc., 1949. The most quoted of all interpretations of the story; Professor West presents a much more simplified interpretation in his University of Minnesota pamphlet on Miss Porter, pp. 9-11.

———. "Katherine Anne Porter and 'Historic Memory,' " *Hopkins Review,* VI (Fall, 1952), 16-27. Reprinted in Louis D. Rubin, Jr., and Robert D. Jacobs. *Southern Renascence.* Baltimore: The Johns Hopkins Press, 1953, pp. 278-89. A sensitive study, especially good on "Old Mortality," but marred by the assumption that Miss Porter was, by birth, a Roman Catholic.

———. *Katherine Anne Porter.* Minneapolis: University of Minnesota Press, 1963. Utilizes much material from the two articles above; a good introduction to Miss Porter's works. After publication, Miss Porter informed Professor West that the stories of her Catholic girlhood were erroneous, and a correction has been added to more recent copies of the pamphlet.

WIESENFARTH, BROTHER JOSEPH. "Illusion and Allusion: Reflections in 'The Cracked Looking-Glass,' " *Four Quarters,* XII (November 1962), 30-37. A fresh look at a neglected story, tracing influences of James, Joyce, and Tennyson; an attempt to determine "the function and meaning of the mirror symbol."

WILSON, EDMUND. "Katherine Anne Porter," *Classics and Commercials.* New York: Farrar, Straus and Co., 1950. Reprinted from *The New Yorker,* XX (September 30, 1944), 72-75. A curious piece of criticism from Wilson, for he admits that he could not "take hold of her work in any of the obvious ways."

YOUNG, VERNON A. "The Art of Katherine Anne Porter," *American Thought—1947.* New York: The Gresham Press, 1947, pp. 223-38. Reprinted from *The New Mexico Quarterly,* XV (Autumn, 1945), 326-41. A thoughtful criticism of her stories.

with attention to her themes, style, and psychological probings. She is "the most flawless realist of her generation. . . ."

YOUNGBLOOD, SARAH. "Structure and Imagery in Katherine Anne Porter's 'Pale Horse, Pale Rider,'" *Modern Fiction Studies,* V (Winter, 1959), 344-52. Now a standard reading of this story.

5. *Criticism of* Ship of Fools

AUCHINCLOSS, LOUIS. "Bound for Bremerhaven—and Eternity," New York *Herald-Tribune Books,* April 1, 1962, pp. 3, 11. A completely favorable review.

BEDFORD, SYBILLE. "Voyage to Everywhere," *The Spectator,* November 16, 1962, pp. 763-64. One of the few favorable English reviews.

BODE, CARL. "Katherine Anne Porter, Ship of Fools," *Wisconsin Studies in Contemporary Literature,* III (Fall, 1962), 90-92. "*Ship of Fools* is an honest, disheartening book. It is not over-written or over-blown. Quite the reverse: it has been revised downward. Its basic image is old but as the author develops it, it becomes modern and more complex. I do not believe that *Ship of Fools* reaches the heights of Miss Porter's earlier work but I am sure it will find a place, if a small one, in our literary histories."

v. BORCH, HERBERT. " 'Die Deutschen sind allzumal grausam, boese und fanatisch"/Dokument des Hasses: K. A. Porters 'Narrenschiff,'" *Die Welt,* June 9, 1962.

BRANT, SEBASTIAN. *The Ship of Fools.* Translated and with introduction and commentary by Edwin H. Zeydel. New York: Dover Publications, Inc., 1962. Also reproduces the original woodcuts.

"Das Narrenschiff," *Der Spiegel,* September 12, 1962, pp. 74, 77. Nationalistic criticism in the German version of *Time.*

DE VRIES, PETER. "Nobody's Fool (A Character or Two Overlooked in Miss Katherine Anne Porter's Shipload)," *The New Yorker,* XXXVIII (June 16, 1962), 28-29. A rather wicked satire on Miss Porter and the long parturition of *Ship of Fools.*

FADIMAN, CLIFTON. "Ship of Fools," *Book-of-the-Month Club News* (April, 1962), pp. 2-4. "She is a simon-pure novelist, a professional, always in command of her complex material."

HEILMAN, ROBERT B. "Ship of Fools: Notes on Style," *Four Quarters,* XII (November, 1962), 46-55.

HENDRICK, GEORGE. "Hart Crane Aboard the Ship of Fools: Some Speculations," *Twentieth Century Literature,* IX (April, 1963), 3-9. Appears, in different form, in Chapter 5.

HICKS, GRANVILLE. "Voyage of Life," *Saturday Review,* XLV (March 31, 1962), 15-16. "Although we have known her people uncommonly well, we watch unconcernedly as, in the curiously muted ending, they drift away from us."

HORTON, PHILIP. *Hart Crane: The Life of an American Poet.* New York: The Viking Press, 1957, pp. 283-87. Miss Porter's own account of "Crane's spiritual disorder and anguish." Should be read with Crane's letters to and about Miss Porter.

KAUFFMANN, STANLEY. "Katherine Anne Porter's Crowning Work," *The New Republic,* April 2, 1962, pp. 23-25. A careful reading; far less favorable than most of the early reviews. Objects that the novel is a portrait gallery, not the allegory it promised to be, that it lacks profundity, and that the treatment of the Jew "gives too mean and sullen a picture."

LEVITAS, GLORIA. "Katherine Anne Porter at the 'Y': 'I Wrote the Book I Meant To,'" New York *Herald-Tribune,* October 11, 1962 (Rowalt clipping book). A brief account of her appearance at the "Y" and a resumé of her writing career. "Summing up her career, she says, 'I don't regret one day of my life. I spent a lot of time just living. I never meant to write a novel—and now some people tell me I haven't written one. Well, that's their privilege.'"

LIETZMANN, SABINA. "Eine Allegorie von der deutschen Gefahr/Der neue amerikanische Bestseller 'Narrenschiff' von Katherine Anne Porter," *Frankfurter Allgemeine Zeitung,* July 16, 1962, p. 16. A political reading of the novel.

"The Longest Journey," *Newsweek* (International Edition), April 2, 1962, pp. 58-59. "If there is one central theme it may be said to be the terrifying inability of most of these people to extend any comprehension of mind, magnanimity of feeling, or compassion of heart to those around them."

Moss, HOWARD. "No Safe Harbor," *The New Yorker,* XXXVIII (April 28, 1962), 165-73. "Miss Porter is a moralist, but too good a writer to be one except by implication. Dogma in 'Ship of Fools' is attached only to dogmatic characters. There is not an ounce of weighted sentiment in it. Its intelligence lies not in the profundity of its ideas but in the clarity of its viewpoint; we are impressed not by what Miss Porter says but by what she knows."

MUHLEN, NORBERT, "Deutsche, wie sie im Buche Stehen," *Der Monat,* December, 1962, pp. 38-45. An unfavorable review in a liberal German journal.

"On the Good Ship Vera," *The Times Literary Supplement,* November 2, 1962, p. 837. Representative of much of the English criticism.

PAECHTER, HEINZ. "Miss Porters neue Kleider/Missverstaendnisse um einen amerikanischen Bestseller," *Deutsche Zeitung,* October 13-14, 1962.

Selected Bibliography

POMPEN, FR. AURELIUS. *The English Versions of The Ship of Fools.*
London: Longmans, Green and Co., 1925. A detailed study of
this complex subject.

SCHORER, MARK. "We're All on the Passenger List," New York *Times
Book Review*, April 1, 1962, pp. 1, 5. Especially good in
discussion of her use of Brant.

SOLOTAROFF, THEODORE. " 'Ship of Fools' & the Critics," *Commentary*,
34 (October, 1962), 277-86. A slashing attack.

SOUTHERN, TERRY. "Recent Fiction, Part I: 'When Film Gets
Good....'" *The Nation* CXCV (November 17, 1962), 330.
"*Ship of Fools* is to be considered a good novel, but only by
persons unaware of present possibilities or new demands . . .; it
has been done before, so what is the point?"

"Speech After Long Silence," *Time* (International Edition), April 6,
1962, p. 67. "Novelist Porter's implication is clear, and it is
the larger import of her extraordinary screed: all passages of
the world's voyage are dismal, and the entente of ignorance
and evil is forever in command."

TAUBMAN, ROBERT. "A First-Class Passenger," *The Statesman*, November 11, 1962 (Rowalt clipping book). "The ship of fools is
a big, worn, rather empty idea but Katherine Anne Porter
doesn't mind playing it up." Completely unfavorable review.

Untitled note on $50,000 advertising budget for *Ship of Fools*,
Publishers Weekly, May 21, 1962 (Rowalt clipping book).

WEBER, BROM, ed. *The Letters of Hart Crane 1916-1932.* New York:
Hermitage House, 1952. Letters detailing the destruction of the
Crane-Porter friendship provide source material for several
scenes in *Ship of Fools*. Miss Porter's account in Horton's
biography should be read, too.

WESCOTT, GLENWAY. "Katherine Anne Porter," *Book-of-the-Month
Club News* (April, 1962), pp. 5-7. Appeared in an expanded
version in "Katherine Anne Porter: The Making of a Novel,"
Atlantic Monthly, CCIX (April, 1962), 43-49; appeared in
another version in "Katherine Anne Porter Personally," *Images
of Truth.* New York: Harper & Row, 1962, pp. 25-58. New
"story material" about Miss Porter and high praise for *Ship
of Fools.*

WILSON, ANGUS. "The Middle-Class Passenger," *The Observer*, October 28, 1962, p. 27. Charges the novel is "middlebrow."

ZINNSER, HANS. *As I Remember Him.* Boston: Little, Brown, 1940.
Contains recollections of Hart Crane.

Index

Index